Barriers to Belief

Barriers to Belief

Steps to a Stronger Faith

Nigel McCulloch

DARTON · LONGMAN + TODD

First published in 1994 by
Darton, Longman and Todd Ltd
1 Spencer Court
140–142 Wandsworth High Street
London SW18 4JJ

ISBN 0–232–52060–7

A catalogue record for this book is available
from the British Library

Cover design by Sarah John

Phototypeset by Intype, London
Printed and bound in Great Britain by
Redwood Books, Trowbridge, Wiltshire

Contents

Preface

This book pretends to be no more than it is: a straightforward attempt to tackle head on people's genuine doubts and questions about faith and the Church; and to explore ways in which some of the obstacles can be overcome.

During this Decade of Evangelism it is hoped that more people will consider seriously the claims of Christianity. What I have written is partly a protest against the unthinking fundamentalism and superficial user-friendliness to which they may find themselves exposed. Alas, these are all too often perceived to be the hallmarks of modern Anglican evangelism.

These chapters do not provide trite answers. Although my personal position on most of the matters raised is the traditional one, that position has been reached only after carefully thinking and praying through the issues involved. There have certainly been moments of doubt. But, as Tennyson's *In Memoriam* observes:

> There lives more faith in honest doubt
> Believe me, than in half the creeds.

I dedicate this book to those people who question and doubt, to enquirers on the fringe, to confirmation candidates, church-wardens, lay leaders, congregations and house groups. Among them I pray that discussion will be stimulated, faith deepened and witness renewed.

* * *

Just as I reached the writing of the last chapter, my mother died.

Her cheerful witness in the face of obstacles in her life drew many people, young and old, to faith, and I remain ever grateful to her for her part in nurturing mine.

My chaplain, Roy Clements, and my secretary, Anne Blackburn have as always been a great encouragement to me and helped me, at a difficult time, to write more cogently.

But it is my wife, Celia, and my family who have paid the price of seeing me so little over the period of writing. I have been greatly blessed by their understanding, love and patience.

Bishop's Lodge, Wakefield
Feast of Corpus Christi 1994

1

Some Barriers and
the Existence of God

The stories of the shepherds and the wise men coming to Jesus can be seen as allegories of how people make the journey of faith. There are those for whom, like the shepherds, it happens quickly and the message is clear. But for many, perhaps for most, it is the experience of the wise men which rings true: the longer journey of searching and questioning. It is for the latter group that I have written this book.

Plenty of attractively produced and simple presentations of the Christian faith have been published which provide neatly packaged answers to every question. But, in my experience as a university chaplain, parish priest and now bishop, I have found that such presentations rarely meet the inner needs of those who are really searching.

People sometimes mock the Church for taking refuge behind the word 'mystery'. In fact that is an example of the Church being honest. Far more is gained by working hard at a problem, than by just guessing the answer and getting it right first time. Genuine exploration is more likely to gain respect for the truth and authority of the Church's beliefs than unthinking platitudes.

In my own spiritual journey I have been described as an 'evangelical catholic with an enquiring mind'! Certainly what I valued when my faith was first nurtured was a healthy mixture of Anglo-Catholic worship and teaching, evangelical Bible studies, and discussion groups on *Honest to God* – the book by Bishop John Robinson, who was asking in the 1960s some of the questions Bishop David Jenkins has been asking more recently.

Perhaps that was a genuine Anglican upbringing – drawing together the best in each strand of the traditions which make up our Church. Nevertheless, I remain traditional in my beliefs – which are the stronger for having been rigorously tested. For it to remain fresh and vibrant, our faith needs constantly to be tested by the experiences and questions of life.

Growing media interest in religious questions

It is sometimes said that theologians spend blameless lives answering questions that no one is actually asking! This book attempts to face up to questions people really are asking. In the twelve month period to mid–1994, the Church of England's Communications Unit recorded an 80% increase in enquiries from the media. Lambeth Palace reported a similar growth. Inevitably, the issues surrounding the ordination of women to the priesthood accounted for much of the interest, but by no means all of it.

The fact is that the Christian Church, its belief and practice, occupies more column inches in newspapers than at any time in living memory. The press is engaged in a fierce battle for circulation figures, so editors are especially conscious of the need to provide material which matches their readers' interests.

That means it is likely that religious matters which gain coverage are matters of genuine fascination and concern to the readers. Furthermore, the increase in reports and articles is not confined to one style of newspaper or programme. Editors and producers seem to be reflecting questions which the general population have about faith – even in what is often described as a secular and pagan society.

This heightened media interest in matters religious could not come at a better time. Launched in 1991, the current Decade of Evangelism is to the Church what their International Year was for the disabled: it is about creating awareness and altering attitudes.

Many Christians find it very difficult to articulate their faith. Yet, all baptised members of God's Church are charged at their baptism: 'Do not be ashamed to confess the faith of Christ crucified.' Why do so many Christians shrink from doing so? Part of the answer is natural shyness, but even if we could break through our own shyness barrier, most of us have little idea what to say about our beliefs – especially to those who are asking questions and need help to overcome the obstacles that are blocking their path to faith. There are barriers everywhere – for Christians and non-Christians alike!

That is why I have written this book for church members as well as enquirers. We are all on a journey of exploration. In looking at some of the issues which make belief difficult, my intention is best summed up in the words of the great St Anselm: I shall try to the best of my ability not so much to show you something as to search with you.

Barriers to belief

There is a deep yearning on the part of many people to ask sharp and honest questions about faith. We must not overlook the capacity of the general public to think complex thoughts about God and the mysteries of life and death.

For over two years I have carefully studied the media's coverage of religious matters in the UK, especially in the press. The following subjects, often presented as barriers to belief, have achieved significant amounts of column inches:

- The apparent confusion, not least within the Church, about Jesus' birth and resurrection – leading to questions about the credibility of his message and his claims in relation to God.
- The seeming preoccupation of the Church with internal wrangling about the nature of its ministry and the seriousness of its financial troubles – clouding its message and feeding accusations of hypocrisy.
- The increasingly significant place of other faiths in this country – encouraging questions about the relationship

of Christianity to other beliefs, and the regularly voiced opinion that basically all religions are the same.

- The continuing and obvious presence of suffering and evil in the world – raising questions about God which Christianity is perceived as being unable to answer, and pointing to a moral vacuum which the Church is thought not to be filling.

- The dominant position of science – resulting in widespread dismissal of the miraculous, and in doubt about the relevance of the Bible; and an increase in major ethical issues to be faced, such as genetic engineering and euthanasia.

- The evidence from death notices and obituaries of the way in which our culture has marginalised death from being a normal event which took place in the heart of home life – and the weakening of the Christian message of judgement, hope and the life beyond.

Confusion about God?

The questions of the existence of God is also a favourite topic for newspapers. A survey published in 1993, by the distinguished Chicago-based researcher Professor Andrew Greeley, shows that almost 70% of British people believe in God. A similar pattern is consistently reproduced in other surveys about belief in this country. The professor comments: 'It is the reverse of everything that the theories of secularisation and religious decline lead us to anticipate. God is not dead, but alive – even in Britain!'

But that may be too rosy a conclusion. Large numbers may believe in God, but that does not mean they feel God is important to their lives. Furthermore, 30% of the population does not have a belief in God. That almost certainly means that in most communities and families there will be agnostics (unable to decide whether God exists or not) or atheists (sure there is no God). G K Chesterton once said that when people stop believing in God they don't believe in nothing – they believe in anything!

But here we come up against a problem of language. What do we mean by God? Some theists and some atheists define God with the same words! Without definitions, statistics about people's belief in God are not that helpful. For example, members of the ultra liberal Sea of Faith Network might well reply to such a survey that they believe in God; but they would then add that God exists only in their minds. For such non-realists, nothing exists outside human language. David Hart's recent book *Faith in Doubt*, in which he explores how it is possible to maintain Christian doctrine and practice when no longer believing in a 'God out there' has been widely recognised as an outstanding contribution to the debate on non-realism and Christian belief.

Much publicity was also given by the newspapers to the Revd Anthony Freeman, an Anglican priest, following publication of his book, *God in Us*, and his removal by his bishop from his diocesan and parish roles. He claims that, whilst valuing religious impulses and prayer, he does not believe in the Christian God – and feels released from an oppressive faith to one which now brings him freedom and joy. Commenting on all this, Walter Schwarz of *The Guardian* wrote: 'The plain fact is that Christians are in total confusion about God.'

But that is not new. In the medieval Church there were substantial disputes about God and the supernatural. The problem about the current views of some of the Sea of Faith is that they provide such a minimal interpretation of belief in God that it amounts to saying God does not exist at all.

Can God's existence be proved?

Here is a major barrier. Can we prove that God exists? The answer to that is simple: No!

Although the Bible points out the greatness of God in the universe, it makes no attempt to set out proofs for God's existence. (Even the reference in the Psalms to the fool who 'has said in his heart that there is no God' is not about denying the existence of God on intellectual grounds. It is to do with the fool's behaviour and denial of God's commandments.)

Some famous Christians have tried to prove that God exists. St Anselm, writing in the eleventh century, produced his 'ontological' argument (from the Greek word meaning 'being'). God, he said, is 'that than which nothing greater can be conceived'. If he did not exist he would not be the greatest conceivable being!

St Thomas Aquinas, writing in the thirteenth century, produced five arguments for the existence of God – the most famous being the 'cosmological' and 'teleological' arguments (from the Greek words meaning 'order' and 'purpose'). There must be a First Cause to everything – and that is God. And, because there is evidence of design and purpose in the world, there must be a Creator.

One of the best known illustrations, based on the design argument, is the story of the watch. A man was walking across a moor, and came across a watch lying on the ground. He picked it up. He had never seen a watch before. He looked at the hands moving around the dial in an orderly way. He opened the watch and saw its wheels, cogs, levers, springs and jewels. Then he discovered he could make the watch go by winding it – and that the whole complex machinery moved in a clearly predetermined pattern. He thought to himself: I have found a watch, so somewhere there must be a watchmaker. This then led the man to think about the world; and how, more accurately than any watch, the tides ebb and flow, the seasons pass in unvarying succession, the planets never leave their courses, and so on. That must mean, he argued, that there is a maker of the world too.

But for many people, the old argument from design was destroyed by Darwin's theory of evolution – though there developed from that the more sophisticated view that although God did not make things, he made them make themselves.

The arguments from cause and design still attract thoughtful presentation. Dr Patrick Dixon, writing in the 'Faith and Reason' column in *The Independent*, noted that as we study the formation of human life in the womb, the mystery of the last moments of earthly existence, or the majestic appearance of the galaxies in space, it becomes obvious to most people that there must be a God, a prime mover, an originator, a cause. 'And if a prime mover, then a God who creates with exquisite detail and care, one who has designed conscious, caring, ethically aware, spiritual beings capable of the deepest thoughts and relationships with himself.'

Perhaps the most effective way of arguing from design in the late twentieth century is on the basis that the universe is intelligible to human minds – thanks to the continuing advances of scientific exploration.

Nor must the moral argument of God's existence be overlooked: that, whether people acknowledge it or not, their conscience and sense of moral values point to the existence of a personal moral creator.

Some arguments, though, verge on eccentricity. Bishop Berkeley, an eighteenth-century Irishman, put forward the view that if there were no God, material objects would have to leap into being whenever we looked at them! This quirky idea led to famous limericks by Ronald Knox – based on a tree standing in the courtyard of an Oxford college.

> There was a young man who said, 'God
> Must think it exceedingly odd
> If he finds that this tree
> Continues to be
> When there's no-one about in the Quad.'

> Dear Sir:
> Your astonishment's odd:
> I am always about in the Quad.
> And that's why the tree
> Will continue to be,
> Since observed by
> Yours faithfully,
> GOD!

The truth is that God can not be measured or analysed. No-one has ever produced a totally convincing proof that God exists. The reason is that God is not a theorem to be proved, but a person to be met.

That is why the Bible deals not with the question of God's existence, but with the fact of his nearness. Michael Ramsey, former Archbishop of Canterbury, once began a talk on God by saying: 'I have come to tell you what is going on inside you . . . There is a space within each one of us that only God can fill.'

But, sadly, many people have squeezed God out of that space. God may be allowed to exist by 70% of the population, but most of them keep him at arm's length – and in so doing trivialise him. 'We are doing God next year', wrote a schoolgirl to the Church of England's Communications Unit. 'Please send all details and pamphlets.'!

As for the remaining 30%, the biggest problem for the atheists is their own existence and genes, whilst the biggest problem for agnostics is their own knowledge.

Glimpses of the divine

In a recent sermon, Cardinal Hume said that, for him, it was the very limitation of all that we see around us which led him to conclude the existence of One who is without any limitations. To acknowledge this transcendence is to recognise that at the heart of our experience of the world and of ourselves lies a mystery. 'To speak of God is to encounter a mystery', he said, 'a reality that we can never fully understand, nor indeed discover for ourselves. The human mind strains as it goes unaided in search of God. It will inevitably be so, for the existence of God is neither clear nor obvious. We cannot know him as we would a friend. He is within our reach yet beyond our grasp.'

There are, however, glimpses of God's glory which we may experience from time to time. I have myself known such glimpses when I have seen beautiful sunsets across the Irish Sea from my childhood home near Liverpool. Like others, I have sensed God's presence on mountain tops in the Lake District and in Austria. Then there are those moments, which I have certainly known, when his love touches us in such a way that we are given the hidden strength to cope with a personal problem or tragedy – and find out for ourselves that 'underneath are the everlasting arms'.

On returning from his solo circumnavigation of the world, Chay Blyth, advised atheists to go sailing single-handed for a few weeks. 'No-one will ever say to me there is no God without my remembering these situations. It strengthened every part of me, deepened every perception and gave me a new awareness of that power outside man which we call God.'

Monica Furlong was quoted in *The Tablet* describing a lunch hour experience in London. It was an August day, quite warm but cloudy, with the sun glaringly, painfully bright behind the clouds. She had a strong sense that something was about to happen and sat on a seat in the garden of Lincoln's Inn waiting for whatever it was to occur. The sun behind the clouds grew brighter and brighter, the clouds assuming a fascinating shape. Then although no word was uttered, she felt herself spoken to. 'I was aware of being regarded by love, of being wholly accepted, accused, forgiven, all at once.' She said that she experienced in that moment the greatest joy she had known in her life. 'I felt I had been born for this moment and had marked time till it occurred.'

It would be a mistake, however, to think that God can be glimpsed only through that kind of experience. It is important to remember that every time we meet someone we can learn a little bit more about God. The reason for that is because every one of us is made in the image of God.

However, each of us has marred that image. From that it follows that we will know most about God from the one in whom God's image has not been marred – that is Jesus Christ. It is he who is the key to making God completely real for ourselves and our world. For, as he told his followers: 'He who sees me sees the Father.'

That is why, in trying to find God, it is important to read the gospels; and to take the time to hear them calling to us through the love of Jesus. Cardinal Hume put it beautifully in a Christmas address:

Read the gospels, and allow God to whisper in your minds and into your hearts words that can have a profound effect on the way we think and act. He will find us if we listen to his voice calling to us through the fog that often surrounds us, a kind of cloud of unknowing, and above the noise that muffles his call. But we must stop from time to time, make space in the day, and especially in the mind, and ask him to make us aware of his presence. When he does, it is the language of love that becomes the only appropriate one. When that happens we have discovered true religion.

FOR REFLECTION

1 Which of the barriers to belief mentioned are obstacles for you? Are there others?
2 Does it help to say that, although God can not be proved, he can be met?

Christmas, Virgin Birth and Incarnation

'The curtain of the temple was torn in two.' According to Luke that happened just before Jesus died. The curtain hid from view the Holy of Holies, the symbolic focus of God's presence. No-one was allowed into it except the High Priest; and even he went in only once a year, on the Day of Atonement. So what Luke is telling us is that, when Jesus died, the barrier blocking the way to God's presence was removed. The curtain which had hidden God was torn apart as a result of the birth, life and death of Jesus.

But how do we know that Jesus really lived? How much of the Christmas story is fairy-tale? Is any of it true? Was Jesus more than just a brilliant teacher? Was he both divine and human? Did he rise from the dead? What does it all mean? And what does it matter?

There can be no serious doubt that Jesus was born, lived, and was crucified in Jerusalem nearly two thousand years ago. The Roman historian Tacitus, in his Annals, mentions Christ's execution. The Jewish historian Josephus, also writing at the end of the first century, refers to 'Jesus who was called the Messiah'. About the same time, Suetonius writes of 'Chrestus'.

The New Testament records were written mostly between AD 40 and AD 100. That was within the lifetime of many of those who had known and heard Jesus, and who were close companions of Mary, his mother. Mark's Gospel, probably the earliest, is thought to be a summary of the preaching of Peter. In the second century, a writer called Papias noted: 'Mark, who was Peter's interpreter, wrote down accurately, though not in order, all that he recollected of what Christ had said or done.'

No reputable scholar denies the authenticity and integrity of the evidence that Jesus existed.

Christmas – fact or fiction?

More people go to church at Christmas than at any other time in the year. Millions of people all over the world listen every Christmas Eve to the famous festival of carols and lessons broadcast from King's College, Cambridge. There are those who say that Christmas really begins when they hear the unaccompanied voice of the young choirboy sing the first verse of 'Once in Royal David's City'.

But does all this help in the journey of faith? Or do the sentimental carols and nostalgia act more as a barrier than as a way to belief? The Bible records that the very first thing Mary did to Jesus was to wrap him up. Of course that was the natural thing to do with a baby. But her action is a symbolic reminder that people have been wrapping Jesus up ever since – not least in churchiness and sentimentality – in such a way that the true meaning of the Christmas message can become obscured.

The deep truths get lost behind superficial headlines: Were there three kings? Was there a star? What about the shepherds and angels? In an age which seeks to question everything, people do wonder: is it true? Increasingly they suspect it is not, but they do not want to spoil the fairy-tale. In fact, ironically, the more secular and pagan our society becomes, the more angry people get when the details of the story are questioned! Faith has become for many people a matter of sentimentality and nostalgia.

There are those who are culturally so far removed from Christianity that they can comment as reported in the newspapers: 'The Church again. Now it's trying to get in on Christmas!' One parent complained after a school nativity play that it was unfair the baby was always a boy!

But the views of most were probably well reflected in a *Daily Mirror* leader: 'Jesus was not just any baby and few of us –

Christians and non-Christians alike – will believe that his arrival in the world was just an ordinary birth. Christmas would not be Christmas without all the angels, the shepherds, the three wise men and the rest of the cast of the most beautiful story ever told.'

It is important to read the Bible stories themselves and not rely on fairy-tale versions of them. In the past two years many column inches in the press have been filled with arguments about seeming discrepancies in the gospel stories, as well as speculation on the date of Christmas, and the existence of the star and the three kings.

Matthew never mentions three kings! He writes about an unspecified group of wise men. Subsequent tradition has turned them into kings, said there were three, and has even given them names – Balthazar, Melchior and Caspar. But the only three-some in Matthew is the gifts – gold, frankincense and myrrh. People such as Matthew describes, however, were well known at that time: combining an expertise in astrology, astronomy and theology, they were seekers after truth who often tested out their intuition by making hazardous journeys.

Did they follow a star? Matthew is clear that the star was important for the wise men. There have been various contenders for a spectacular astronomical happening around that time. For example, on 17 September in the year 7 BC there was a triple conjunction of Jupiter and Saturn in the constellation of Pisces, and some astronomers believe this might have been the Bethlehem 'star'. Others have suggested it might have been the tailed comet which Chinese astronomers observed for seventy days in 5 BC. But no one knows for sure.

Was Jesus born on 25 December? He was probably born at some point between 8 BC, when the Emperor Augustus ordered his tax census, and 4 BC, when King Herod is thought to have died. But if the birth really was in December, then it is unlikely that the shepherds would have been out in the fields: it would have been too cold! The month for rounding up the flocks was September, and then they stayed with the sheep overnight to protect them from wild animals and from wandering off. The date of 25 December may have been chosen later on because of the Church's wish to replace the pagan feast of the birth of the unconquered sun with a Christian festival, and there is no doubt that Christmas was being observed on that date by AD 354. However, some scholars argue that the observance of 25 December as Christmas goes back even earlier – before AD 274 when the Emperor Aurelian imposed the sun festival.

What about the discrepancies in the gospel stories? According to Luke, the Holy Family travelled to Bethlehem for taxation purposes, were denied a room at the inn, and after the birth went back to Nazareth. But Matthew seems to suggest that they were already living in Bethlehem, that Jesus was born in a house, and that they ran away to Egypt to escape Herod.

Another problem seems to be raised by the mention of Quirinius as governor. When he held office, Herod had been dead for eleven years. However, the Greek can be translated to mean 'before Quirinius was governor' – which does solve that particular difficulty.

Many of the inconsistencies between the gospel stories may arise from the concern of the writers to see the birth of Jesus in Old Testament terms. For example, the old prophecies said that the Messiah would be from the House of David and be born in Bethlehem. The story of the wise men and the star is an echo of the prophecy of Balaam in the Book of Numbers that a star would rise out of Jacob. The cruelty of Herod would have reminded them of the bullying of Pharaoh. The gospel writers were not intending to write historical biography as we know it. They would have felt it very important to set Jesus' origins against the background of Old Testament expectations. It does not follow, however, that the gospel stories of Christmas are untrue.

In Middle Eastern tradition such events were handed down by word of mouth in what, again and again, has been shown to be amazingly accurate detail. The Christmas stories as we have received them in the gospels were told near enough to the event to have been founded on oral tradition based on fact. Although in our scientific age, angelic choirs lighting up the skies seem to belong more to fairy-stories than reality, we have to remember that this sort of picture language was at that time a recognised way of saying that God was in it all.

In any case, we would be wise not to be too dismissive, even of angels. The Greek word means 'messenger', and, as Bishop Rowan Williams said: 'The idea that there may be in the universe other kinds of intellectual beings apart from ourselves, and that there may be connections between us and them, is not silly.'

Many people are helped by the poetry and mystery of these beautiful stories to draw nearer to the meaning of Christmas, although *The Daily Telegraph* was absolutely right to reiterate that the truth of Christianity does not depend on their details. That is not to say, however, that the stories can be rubbished as implausible or fictitious. Professor William Frend, a leading Church historian, gave a telling reminder in *The Guardian* that although the gospels were not written as history, that does not mean their writers put down historical impossibilities. 'Before they dismiss the story of Jesus' birth as a legend created by early Christian communities, critics should try to see the events through the eyes of the people living at the time. Then they might talk less tedious nonsense.'

Was it a virgin birth?

For many thinking people, one of the most difficult features of the Christmas story to believe in, especially in a scientific age, is the Virgin Birth (which more accurately should be called the Virgin Conception). A recent survey showed that a quarter regular churchgoers do not believe in it. So Bishop David Jenkins was speaking for a lot of deeply committed Christians, as well as those outside the faith who find this a barrier to belief, when he said: 'I would not put it past God to arrange a Virgin Birth if he wanted to, but I very much doubt if he did.'

Indeed, for many Christians the Virgin Birth, often used now to emphasise the real divinity of Jesus, takes away the idea of his real humanity. It is important that Jesus is fully human as well as fully divine.

The particular questions raised by the Virgin Birth, in relation to whether it happened or not, range from the mainly biological to the deeply theological. First, virgins do not have babies! Professor R J Berry, of London University's Genetics Department, explained in *The Independent* that male babies for virgins present a particular difficulty. The technical name for virgin birth is parthenogenesis, and it occurs in bees and greenfly. For a human to be born in this way, the baby would need a Y-chromosome.

However, according to Professor Berry, a virgin birth is not completely beyond rational bounds. Unfertilised rabbit and mouse eggs can be stimulated by chemical or physical shocks to develop into apparently normal embryos. Although most of these die as early embryos, at least one parthenogenetic rabbit is said to have been born alive. Human eggs will also respond to shocks in a similar way. Furthermore, the fact that a woman has no Y-chromosome to contribute is not such a complete barrier as once thought. Professor Berry has shown that if an ovum in a woman with a particular type of chromosomal mutation develops without fertilisation, the result could be a boy born to a virgin. He concluded: 'The biological mechanisms exist . . . it would be improper in the light of our knowledge of genetics and embryology to say virgin births can never happen.'

But does that really help? How important anyway is the Virgin Birth within the beliefs of Christianity? Professor Keith Ward has said: 'God could have become incarnate without being born of a virgin . . . So it is possible to believe that Jesus is the son of God without accepting the Virgin Birth.' Although it forms part of the Creed, there is no indication from the early centuries that belief in the Virgin Birth was used actually as a proof to support the divinity of Christ. Does this mean the validity of the Christian faith does not depend on it, and that it need not be seen as a barrier to belief? I believe that to be so – even though I personally do accept the Virgin Birth.

In his recent and well-reviewed book *The Womb and the Tomb*, Bishop Hugh Montefiore argues that if Jesus did have a normal human birth, then it is most likely that he was conceived during the betrothal of Joseph and Mary; and, he adds, such an occurrence seems quite compatible with God's gracious action of Incarnation. Nevertheless, he is struck by the way Matthew almost takes the Virgin Birth for granted; and he finds it difficult to believe that the Christmas stories in Luke are his own invention – rather than being based on what may well have been reliable sources. There is no doubt that, if God wished to do so, he could have miraculously overridden the normalities of human reproduction. 'I cannot therefore deny the possibility of Virginal Conception, but . . . I cannot affirm it. I have to remain agnostic about its historicity, although of course I enthusiastically accept the doctrinal truths underlying it.'

Bishops are expected to be guardians of the faith. Are the views of David Jenkins and Hugh Montefiore backed by the Church of England's House of Bishops? In other words, what is the official line? My own view, as a guardian of the faith but also a searching enquirer, is reflected in the 1986 House of Bishops' statement and exposition, *The Nature of Christian Belief*. This says: 'As regards the Virginal Conception of Our Lord, we acknowledge and uphold belief in it as expressing the faith of the Church of England.' The document continues: 'All of us accept: first, that the belief that Our Lord was conceived in the womb of Mary by the creative power of God the Holy Spirit without the intervention of a human father can be held with full intellectual integrity.' We also say that only this belief, enshrined in the Creeds, can claim to be the teaching of the universal Church.

The document also affirms the truth that, in Christ, God has taken the initiative for our salvation by uniting our human nature with himself, so bringing into being a new humanity.

Incarnation – What does it mean and does it matter?

Perhaps such theological language seems a far cry from the real world of Christmas – when hardship becomes more focused and there are more family break-ups than at any other time in the year. If Christmas is about more than sentimental stories and a virgin birth, how can it be explained in such a way as to lead people to faith in Jesus and help them to be released from stress and tragedy? Can the Christian message of Christmas be explained without enveloping people in the darkness of intellectual obscurity? What on earth does it all mean?

The 'on earth' bit is very important. As the hymn puts it: 'He came down to earth from heaven, who is God and Lord of all.' It is about God identifying with us. That is what matters about Christmas. Lovely though the stories about the Magi and the shepherds may be, they really can be an impediment to understanding the true meaning of the birth of Jesus and how we can be helped by it. That is what Bishop David Jenkins meant – the wrappings do seriously obscure the gift. The Incarnation itself is the true miracle of Christmas – a far greater miracle even than birth to a virgin.

Literally translated, Incarnation means 'enfleshing'. God walked on this earth in human flesh. As Bishop Irenaeus said centuries ago: 'The Word of God, Jesus Christ, on account of his great love for mankind, became what we are in order to make us what he is himself.'

By taking on human form in Bethlehem, God came not only to identify himself with us – but also to rescue us. He identified himself with us in his life and death by entering our worst human experience and by enduring the worst of our mistreatment of one another. In a world characterised by bullying and suffering, God – as Jesus shows him to be – shares in his people's sufferings. But the point is that he does more than that. He rescues us too: The name 'Jesus', in the original Hebrew, means 'God is the one who saves'. God took human form so that he could save us and make it possible for us to come to him. A slogan I saw outside a church one Christmas put it neatly: 'God to the rescue' it said.

The Methodist preacher Leonard Griffith explained the Incarnation by telling a story about a Hindu. For many of those who belong to other faiths, the thought of God becoming a vulnerable baby and growing into a man who was crucified is anathema. Likewise, the Hindu could not believe that Infinite God would become man. One day he came across a colony of ants. He became interested in them, and, as he bent over, his shadow fell across the ant hill. Immediately there was confusion among the insects – workers dropped their burdens, warrior ants came to defend their hill, and panic reigned. As the Hindu man drew back, the sun fell again on the ant hill and order was gradually restored. But as he bent over it again, panic reappeared. Idly, he began to wonder how he could bridge the gap between man and the insect – to show the ants that his drawing near indicated nothing but sympathy and interest. Then he realised that the only way this would be possible would be somehow to become an ant himself, accepting the risks and terrors of life in the sand and grass. Only then could be communicated to the ants the intentions of his human heart. Bent in the dust he had been thinking God's thoughts. Now he understood the meaning of the Incarnation.

The Times, in a leading article for Christmas, described the Incarnation as 'the shocking centre of Christian faith, which dares to claim that in the fragility and contingency of a single human life the Creator knew his creation from the inside'. In a newspaper which that same day published stories of human tragedy from around the world, the true Christmas message was shown to be far removed from sentimental carols and fairy lights: 'God comes into the muck and mire. Part of the carnality of the incarnation is that God comes into the carnage.' The point about Matthew's nativity story, which is so often overlooked, is that it is not just a cosy story about wise men following a star. It is also an uncomfortable and brutal tale about Herod's butchery of children, the massacre of the innocents. In other words God comes down to us where we are. And where we are is in a world of bullets and bombs, a world of tyranny, a world of imprisoning addiction, of depression, loneliness and bereavement. The God of love comes from heaven to the hell which is love distorted into hatred.

As *The Times* article said:

> The truth of Christianity, the truth of Christmas, does not depend on the historicity of the wise men or stars or shepherds, though they may and do speak of its truth, but it does depend on incarnation, that God is love like this, not just a metaphor or way of speaking, but in reality. Such a stupendous affirmation necessarily stretches our language to the limits, and brings us to the adoration where words and even music fail.

FOR REFLECTION

1 What do you like best and least about Christmas?
2 How important for you are the actual details of the Christmas stories? Which speak powerfully to you?
3 Do you believe in the Virgin Birth? Is it essential for a Christian to do so?
4 What is the meaning of the Incarnation – and to what extent is it really about 'muck and mire'?

3

Teaching, the Empty Tomb and Resurrection

'Here is a man who was born in an obscure village, the child of a peasant woman. He worked in a carpenter's shop until he was thirty; then for three years was a travelling preacher. He never wrote a book. He never held public office. He never did any of the things that usually accompany greatness.

'While he was still a young man the tide of popular opinion turned against him. His friends let him down; his enemies put him through a mockery of a trial. He was nailed to a cross between two thieves; and while he was dying his executioners gambled for his cloak. When he was dead his body was laid in a borrowed grave thanks to the pity of a friend.

'Nearly two thousand years have come and gone. Yet all the armies that ever marched, all the navies that were ever built, all the parliaments that ever met, and all the kings that ever reigned, put together, have not affected the life of men and women on this earth as powerfully as has that one solitary life.'

Few would disagree with those famous words of an unknown writer. Jesus has had a greater influence than any other person over the whole course of human history. And Christians would want to say even more than that. In the human life of Jesus long ago, the love of God walked on this earth – and was nailed to a cross. But that is not the end of the story. Jesus is still alive today – and can change the lives of all those who meet him now.

Taking the risk

People often write to newspapers saying what they think Christianity is about. It is usually expressed as 'doing good to others'. But Jesus summed up his teaching differently in a phrase which occurs over 150 times in the gospels: 'the Kingdom of God'. (Matthew, in deference to Jewish sensitivity about using the name of God, uses the phrase 'the Kingdom of Heaven'.)

But what is the Kingdom? When will it come? How is it to be entered? The fact is that Jesus never precisely defined what he meant by the Kingdom of God! The phrase has at least six different meanings in the gospel sayings. Even in his parables the approach is oblique – but those who had 'ears to hear' heard there a stark and subversive message, so risky that in the end it led to crucifixion.

A clue to one aspect of the Kingdom lies in the Lord's Prayer. After the phrase 'thy kingdom come' the prayer continues 'thy will be done'. In other words, when we are doing God's will, the Kingdom is upon us. Indeed a modern translation, instead of beginning the parables with the phrase, 'the kingdom of God is like this . . .', starts with 'God's way is like this . . .'. Those parables make it clear that God's way is something that each of us has to find for ourselves. That, of course, is why it can not be defined exactly. There is a hidden, secret path, which is our own special, individual journey of faith – unlike anyone else's journey. Going on God's way for us is about taking a risk – about being willing to make the attempt to break through the barriers and climb the steps of faith.

There is a famous story about a flock of geese that milled around in a filthy barnyard imprisoned by a high wooden fence. One day a preaching goose came to them. He stood on an old crate and admonished the geese for being content with their confined, earthbound existence. He recounted the exploits of their forefathers who spread their wings and flew the trackless wastes of the sky. He spoke of the goodness of the Creator who had given geese the urge to migrate and the wings to fly. This pleased the geese. They nodded their heads and said: What a splendid sermon, how very good. But one thing they never did. They never did fly. They just went back to their waiting dinner, for the corn was good and the barnyard safe and secure.

As the wise men discovered on their way to Bethlehem, the journey to faith can be hazardous. It requires the readiness to take risks. One day when the children were crowding round Jesus and the disciples were trying to push them away, Jesus told his disciples off and said: 'Let the children come to me. Do not stop them.' And we are told that he took a little child and said: 'Whoever does not receive the kingdom of God as a little child shall not enter it.'

Was Jesus talking about their innocence and obedience, as many commentators seem to think? As a father, I am not entirely convinced that innocence and obedience are necessarily a child's strongest qualities! But I do know that my wife and I often had our hearts in our mouths when our children were small, and we watched their latest daring exploit – up a tree, or down the bannisters, or doing some hair-raising trick on a bike. Small children do not seem to have a sense of danger or fear: in other words, if you are going to get anywhere along God's way then you must take risks just like children. Perfect love casts out fear.

That is what can be offputting about Christian commitment. Being part of God's kingdom may mean giving up safety and security – be that physical, mental or emotional – and venturing into the unknown. That was Jesus' message. It is a message echoed in the often quoted words of Louise Haskins:

> I said to the man who stood at the gate of the year: Give me a light that I might tread safely into the unknown. And he replied: Go out into the darkness and put your hand into the hand of God. That shall be to you better than light and safer than a known way.

Human and divine?

God can be glimpsed in many ways, but the Christian faith claims that it is from Jesus that we can learn fully what God is like. The Christian faith says: If you want to know about God begin with Jesus.

'Who do men say that I am?' asked Jesus. And Peter replied: 'You are the Christ, the Son of the living God.' The disciples did not come to that conclusion easily. It is impossible for us today to imagine how difficult it must have been for Peter to take that first step. Peter was a Jew, brought up to believe in a distant God, and in a Messiah, quite different from Jesus, who would release them from the Romans. Later, in the upper room, Philip said, 'Lord, show us the Father and we shall be satisfied'. Jesus answered: 'Have I been with you so long, and yet you do not know me Philip? He who has seen me has seen the Father.'

That is why Jesus must be at the heart of our search for God: not just because of his teachings about the Kingdom and the brilliant stories he told. Not just because of his miracles or his new commandment to love one another. Not just because of his call to his followers to take up the cross. Not just because of the assurance he gave of salvation in this world and the world to come. What is supremely important is that, in Jesus, God himself walked our path.

As C S Lewis put it: 'The discrepancy between the depth, sincerity and, may I say, the shrewdness of his moral teachings and the rampant megalomania which must lie behind his theological teaching unless he is indeed God, has never been got over.'

Nevertheless, there is sharp questioning and rejection of the divinity of Jesus in recent books which have received wide coverage. A N Wilson, for example, making much of current studies of the Jewish background of Jesus, denies that Jesus was divine. He sees Jesus as merely a Galilean *hasid*, or holy man, who had peculiar insights into man's relationship with God, and charismatic powers of healing. 'Jesus was nothing more, and certainly not divine.'

Similarly, Barbara Thiering hit the headlines with her claim that Jesus was married, had three children, did not die on a cross and continued his ministry into old age! She writes convincingly of how Jesus brought a special kind of personality to his role as a leader of the Essenes. The gospels, she claims, are written in a code she says she has cracked, having found the key in the Dead Sea Scrolls. The controversial Bishop Jack Spong has also written strongly against the divinity of Christ. Other scholars have argued similarly, and many are divided about whether Jesus was in fact viewed by any of his contemporaries as the Messiah. More recently some have linked Jesus to the contemporary Cynics movement.

None of that denies what the Jewish scholar Geza Vermes sees as the appeal of Jesus as a teacher both in his own time and for those outside the Church today. 'The magnetic appeal of the teaching and example of Jesus holds up hope and guidance to those outside the fold of organised religion.'

Dean Tom Wright has shown in his widely acclaimed book *Who was Jesus?* that it is important for us to see the life and teaching of Jesus in its Jewish context. The 'Christ' who is worshipped by the Church must not be separated from the real Jesus who lived in Palestine in the first century, and who died on a cross. Otherwise, he warns, the word 'Jesus' becomes a mere cipher. We can pull or push it this way and that without any control. The trouble then is that 'Jesus' can be invoked to support all kinds of opinions and programmes. 'To prevent this we need serious Jesus-research'. But, as he goes on to point out, the New Testament is resistant to what might be called textual archaeology. It is as if the authors left out all the useful clues for the reconstruction of Jesus' life on purpose! Nevertheless: 'The Jesus of the gospels, precisely as a human being, believed himself called to do things, and to be things, which only make sense if it was God himself who was doing them and being them.'

Crucifixion

Unfortunately a lot of traditional Passiontide devotion cloaks the worshipper in a cocoon of safe piety. One of the redeeming features of many a Good Friday Three Hours Devotion is the intruding, sometimes even subverting, noise of the real world outside. In fact the Passion narratives make abundantly clear the genuinely subversive nature of Jesus. The Sanhedrin was made up of religious people who were not particularly bad, but who felt it their duty to make sure no-one rocked the boat, and that worship in the Temple could carry on as normal. In that they were not much different from a large number of respectable Parochial Church Councils today! They did not like change.

What they faced, as they saw it, was an unmarried, unemployed thirty-year-old who was 'over the top' and who ought to know better. To them he was an anti-establishment 'lefty', roaming around with a bad lot and speaking out against the Pharisees and religious authority. He was subverting the Messianic message and encouraging all the wrong kind of people to celebrate the Kingdom with him: the poor, the crippled the blind – all those who had been squeezed to the margins of society. His idea of the Kingdom was about a great reversal: 'He has put down the mighty from their seat, and has exalted the humble and meek.' No wonder they arranged for him to be put to death. He was causing mayhem in their cosily established religious world. Deep down, they were afraid of him and his higher claim, 'My kingdom is not of this world'.

In a moving Holy Week address, Ian Hislop, the editor of *Private Eye*, said:

> At the age I am now, Jesus' life was finished. He had either completed an extraordinary mission or had been pointlessly and tragically executed. The end is either Christ's last cry of desolation in Luke: 'My God my God why have you forsaken me?' Or it is the certainty of the words: 'Father into your hands I commend my spirit.' I don't know. I've sat in churches thinking this is all rubbish. I've thought the mockers'

thoughts. And at other times I have felt that this is all there is. I don't know. I don't know.

That probably expresses the way a lot of people feel. To get beyond that point does mean taking a risk. After all, the Christian journey is about carrying your cross, and the steps of faith are demanding.

In my own ministry of helping people to come to faith, I have often used a story about Archbishop William Temple whose missions had a great impact on many people's lives. Temple avoided directing his appeal to the emotions, and had none of the tricks of the professional missioner.

On the last night of one of his missions to students the final hymn was being sung. It was 'When I survey the wondrous cross'. Just before the last verse, Temple stopped the singing and said: 'I want you to read over this verse before you sing it. They are tremendous words. If you mean them with all your hearts, sing them as loud as you can. If you don't mean them at all, keep silent. If you mean them even a little, and want to mean them more, sing them very softly.'

It was, said of those present, 'an experience never to be erased from my memory', as two thousand young men and women sang very softly these words:

> Were the whole realm of nature mine,
> That were an offering far too small;
> Love so amazing, so divine,
> Demands my soul, my life, my all.

Resurrection

'Love's redeeming work is done', sings the Church at Easter, and sums up the triumph in the ancient greeting: 'The Lord is risen: He is risen indeed, Alleluia!' The Resurrection of Jesus is at the heart of the Christian gospel. Without it, Christianity makes little sense. As St Paul says very plainly in 1 Corinthians

15: 'If Christ has not been raised, our preaching is useless and so is your faith.'

What is the Resurrection really about? Newspapers have been eager to headline arguments about whether or not the body of Jesus literally rose from the tomb. When the appointment of the new Bishop of Durham was announced, reporters were quick to ask him what he believed about this key issue. Affirming the traditional belief that Jesus did indeed rise from the tomb, he added: 'It is a pity there wasn't a photocall on that day.'

The media frenzy about what happened to the body of Jesus is a distraction, for if the Christian Church gives the impression to the world that that is all Easter is about, then it is in danger of trivialising the faith and diverting attention from the key element of the Resurrection. Some theologians have argued that it is unnecessary and misleading to claim a belief in the empty tomb is essential for Christian faith. That is not a view I share, but I do think it is a mistake to place so much emphasis on the empty tomb that the meaning of the Resurrection is obscured.

The New Testament certainly declares very clearly that the tomb was empty and the body of Christ was raised to life. But the actual mode of the Resurrection remains tantalisingly unclear. His risen body appears to have properties which transcend the earthly body. He appears and disappears. In fact the nature of Christ's resurrected body has always been a puzzle to scholars and a holy mystery to believers. Unfortunately, many Christians either do not know of, or will not admit to, that puzzle and mystery. Inexcusably, many clergy avoid facing up to it.

For the Christian, the significant point is that not only did Jesus rise from the dead on that first Easter Day but he is still alive now. He is alive in all those who know him as their Lord and Saviour, and follow his new commandment to 'love one another' – confronting injustice and alleviating suffering wherever it is in the world.

Yes, the Christian faith is firmly rooted in historical fact; but, as the New Testament theologian Christopher Rowland has perceptively warned: 'Unless the Resurrection means the transformation of the world in actual practice today, it ends up as a tempting ideology which may even blind us to the suffering and injustice of God's world.'

The garden tomb in Jerusalem (though it is probably not the actual site) has on its door the gospel message: 'He is not here. He is Risen.' That is a very important message to all who are entombed by doubt or despair, by buildings and structures – and by cosy personal religion. The Risen Jesus provides the opportunity to be released and to break out from tombs.

Was the tomb empty?

The whole of this section must be seen in the context of all that has been said above. The Easter stories in all four gospels begin with the Empty Tomb. As we noted earlier, St Mark's gospel is thought by some scholars to be a summary of the teaching of St Peter – who was first into the tomb. At least five others are said to have seen it empty that morning. The gospel accounts have some vivid human touches. Running to the tomb, John is faster but more cautious on arrival and just peeps in. Peter, out of breath, typically barges in! What they saw was extraordinary. The body had gone, and the clothes, which had been so carefully and lovingly wrapped round Jesus, were left in such a way that the only possible explanation was that the body had somehow passed through them. The tomb was empty!

Or did the two Marys, and Peter and John, all go to the wrong tomb? If they did, how is that the authorities did not produce the body from the right tomb and silence the disciples? The Greek in the gospel story emphasises that the two Marys had taken a good long look at where Jesus was laid when he was taken from the cross. They knew where the tomb was.

Had the body been stolen? Again, if the authorities had taken it, they would have produced it and soon silenced early Christianity. If thieves had taken it, how can the extraordinary position of the grave clothes and the valuable spices left behind be explained?

Did the disciples hide the body? If so, would they have allowed themselves to be martyred without any of them ever confessing it was all a hoax?

Perhaps Jesus only fainted and then somehow escaped? Well, ask yourself those questions often put to those attracted by that proposition. How could a man who struggled to Calvary, was nailed to the cross for six hours, pronounced dead and speared by the soldiers, then spent three days in a cold tomb without food and attention become so revived that he was able to set himself free from the spice-laden grave clothes, roll away a great stone, pass the guards, and walk miles on pierced and wounded feet – not to mention then impressing the disciples that he was conqueror over death and Prince of Life?

Perhaps most telling of all, how did that dejected group of disciples come to be filled with joy and, in the words of their enemies, start to turn the world upside down, if what they themselves said about the empty tomb was not true?

How else did those rather weak people find the strength to face imprisonment, beatings and martyrdom; how else was Peter's cowardly denial transformed into the courage that led to his own crucifixion? What convinced James, who had thought Jesus mad, to become a great leader of the Church? What changed Thomas from a downcast doubter into a joyful believer? What about a hard-headed business man like Matthew – or an intelligent doctor like Luke – or a down-to-earth fisherman like Andrew? Were they all taken in by a hoax? Had they got it all wrong? Or did the gospel writers really *mean* 'The tomb is empty. The Lord is risen'?

Modern versions of the old arguments against the tomb being empty are popular reading. But as Bishop Richard Holloway concluded in his review of Bishop Spong's book *Resurrection: Myth or Reality?*: 'After a while, the relentless, driving determination to overturn everything believed by most Christians about Easter, including many distinguished scholars, becomes tedious.' In any case, in the first century the word 'resurrection' was understood to mean that a dead person really was alive again, not in some strange non-physical way, but in the sense that there would not be a body in the tomb. Dean Tom Wright put it this way in his riposte to Bishop Spong and others: 'The only reason why the early Christians would have used this word about Jesus – as they did all the time – was that this is what had happened. All the ingenuity of sceptical scholars cannot get round this quite simple world-shattering fact.'

So when the New Testament writers refer to the Resurrection appearances of Jesus which the disciples experienced, they intend us to understand that his body was no longer in the tomb. The risen Jesus is clearly not a ghost. Although he comes to his disciples through locked doors, his body has the marks of his crucifixion – and on another occasion he eats fish.

Sometimes they do not recognise him immediately, yet when they do, they are sure it is him. He is the same but different. It is the same Jesus but he has passed beyond death into another kind of existence in which his body has been transformed.

Bishop Hugh Montefiore puts another viewpoint. He finds the strongest argument against the empty tomb not in the conflicting gospel accounts nor its intrinsic improbability, but a doctrinal consideration. If Jesus was like us in every way except without sin, then why should he be raised to a new form of existence in a way different from that of other people? He quotes his own tutor Professor Geoffrey Lampe, who felt this argument so deeply that it formed one of the main reasons why he did not believe in the empty tomb – although he had a profound conviction about Jesus being raised to life after his physical death, which sustained him during his own terminal illness. Lampe referred to the comfort given through the centuries by Baxter's hymn with its words:

> Christ leads me through no darker rooms
> Than he went through before;
> He that into God's kingdom comes
> Must enter by this door.

He felt that if the story of the empty tomb were true, Christ's door into God's Kingdom would not be ours. Instead we would find ourselves facing another door through which he has never entered: into a darker room which his presence had never lightened.

In fact Montefiore himself is not convinced by that view. Nor am I. It is important to remember that the Empty Tomb is affirmed in all four gospels. The records of Jesus' appearances bear the hallmarks of authentic experiences. The disciples do seem to be convinced of the reality of Jesus, and Paul's powerful testimony, which is dated earlier than the gospels, also rings true. All that adds up to a very strong case in favour of the scriptural witness to the Empty Tomb and the physical Resurrection of Jesus. But that is not proof. There will, therefore, always be people who remain agnostic about, or who do not believe in, the Empty Tomb. It is certainly possible to have that view and still believe in the Resurrection triumph of Jesus over death and sin.

However, that is not my position. I am convinced that on that first Easter Day the tomb was indeed empty. The 1986 House of Bishops' statement, *The Nature of Belief*, declares:

> We recognise that scholarship can offer no conclusive demonstration; and the divergent views to be found among scholars of standing are reflected in the thinking of individual bishops. But all of us accept first, that belief that the tomb was empty can be held with full intellectual integrity; secondly that this is the understanding of the witness of Scripture which is generally received in the universal Church; and thirdly, that this House acknowledges and upholds this belief as expressing the faith of the Church of England and of its historic teaching . . .

Just as the Virgin Birth is a lesser miracle than the Incarnation itself, so the Empty Tomb must not deflect from the greater miracle of the Resurrection. We can learn from the way in which Eastern Churches' icons portray the Resurrection. In the West, medieval paintings of the Resurrection depict Christ invariably stepping out of a tomb, but, in the East, Christ is portrayed as triumphant over the imprisoning powers of darkness.

Indeed, if those early disciples who experienced the Resurrection could speak to us today, might they not say: 'Yes, early on that Sunday morning we did indeed find the tomb empty. That is true. But even more important is the truth that Jesus is still alive with us, still sharing our lives and still talking with us'.

Two thousand years on the Christian Church celebrates the Light of Christ and continues to witness to that truth.

FOR REFLECTION

1. What attracts or frightens you most about Jesus' teaching?
2. Was the tomb empty?
3. What does Easter mean to you?

4

The Church – Hypocritical, Divided, Irrelevant and Exclusive

Many people who are attracted to the picture of Jesus are put off by what they see of the Church. That is true of all denominations – but perhaps, because it is the national, and most visible, Church, such feelings are particularly focused on the Church of England. There is its perceived hypocrisy – pronouncing on poverty while retaining palaces; its internal squabbling – about things which to most people are unimportant issues – and its exclusive role within the life of a nation which for the most part regards it as boring and irrelevant.

Hypocrisy

The Church is thought not to practise what it preaches. That is not new. Even Paul had to write sternly to the Corinthian Church: 'You should be ashamed of yourselves! You have made Christianity the laughing stock of the whole world.' But to condemn the whole Church because many of its members behave in a hypocritical manner would be rather like condemning a hospital because many of its patients are confined to bed. The Church exists for sinners. The hypocrisy of Christians does not invalidate the Christian faith any more than a careless motorist invalidates the invention of the engine.

That the Church has done horrendous things through the centuries is indisputable: pogroms against Jews, crusades against Muslims, executions and burnings of opponents, religious wars, missionary colonialism. It is tragically true that Christianity has often been a source of untold misery, and it is to the shame of generations of Christians that the message of God's love has been so perverted and misused. But it is also true that countless lives have been made happier and more fulfilled because of Christianity; and that the world has been enriched by its many saints, known and unknown.

But do you have to go to church to be a good Christian? There are plenty of people who live good lives which are in harmony with the teachings of Jesus, but who do not belong to a church or even subscribe to its faith. Nevertheless, Jesus made it clear that following him meant being a part of his family – branches of the vine that is the Church. Far too often the Church is thought of as a stone building. In fact, a Christian Church is a group of people – a Church of living stones. The earliest description of what the Church should be like is given in the Acts of the Apostles (2:42): 'They devoted themselves to the apostles' teaching and to the fellowship, to the breaking of bread and to prayer.' Unless faith is shared with others, and unless it is exposed to living and talking with others, religion quickly becomes selfish.

Bishop Geoffrey Paul once said: 'There is no way of belonging to Jesus Christ except by belonging gladly and irrevocably to the glorious ragbag of saints and fatheads who make up the One, Holy and Catholic Church!'

St Teresa of Avila expressed it more beautifully in her meditation:

Christ has no body now on earth but ours
No hands but ours, no feet but ours;
Ours are the eyes through which Christ's compassion is to
    look out on the world
Ours are the feet with which he is to go about doing good
And ours the hands with which he is to bless people now.

Indeed it is precisely because Christ's body on earth now is made up of our hands and feet and eyes that the Church constantly falls short of the ideal and is perceived to be hypocritical. Yet, despite all its obvious failings it still witnesses to the message that Jesus is alive. The Church's continuing strength and vitality, against all odds, is itself evidence of Jesus' Resurrection. And the Church's manifesto is the same as the one Jesus proclaimed at Nazareth (Luke 4): good news to the poor and release for the imprisoned and oppressed.

But all that seems to ring a bit hollow when the Church of England is known to have enormous financial assets – some of which the Church Commissioners notoriously lost in ill-advised property investments. The perception is that the Church of England is very rich, and ought not to need extra money.

The truth is the reverse. If it were not for the income from the largesse of previous generations, the Church could not pay its way. The Church of England is unique in that it provides at least one church building in every parish, and an ordained ministry serving every community. That is an enormous spiritual and physical presence and strength – which no other denomination even attempts to match. But the cost of the upkeep of buildings and the maintenance of a pastoral and missionary ministry falls increasingly on the congregations who, faced with less money from the Church Commissioners to subsidise them, have to give more and more.

The palaces of the past are now mainly functional places of work – with offices and often the equivalent of a flat for the bishop's family. Public rooms and large grounds are used by parishes or administered by trustees to raise money for upkeep. In fact no other institution of comparable significance comes anywhere near to such tight and prudent financial management as the Church of England both nationally and locally. That is why when something does go wrong it makes news.

Indeed, although the Church is sometimes perceived to be hypocritical, the general public's view is that it has considerable integrity in the way it operates, both corporately and individually.

An exclusive poll for *The Daily Express* in early 1994 showed the Church way up above all others in response to the question: Which institution do you feel has helped raise or maintain moral standards? The Church was way ahead again in a similar poll for

The Observer. In *The Daily Express*'s poll, the response to a question about people perceived to have higher moral standards than ordinary people, put the clergy firmly into first place with more than twice as many points as the nearest contenders.

Indeed, for all its perceived wealth, it is the Church of England which has been in the forefront of servanthood in the inner cities. There are few accusations of hypocrisy levelled at the Church in this area – though irritation is expressed by those who feel that the Church of England is over concerned with making political comments. In his Easter sermon in 1994 the Archbishop of Canterbury spoke, in the context of a clear Resurrection message, of the growing gap between rich and poor. This led to a widely reported outburst by Ann Widdicombe MP, who expressed her relief as a new convert to Roman Catholicism that she had been listening to the Cardinal preaching the Resurrection message rather than the Archbishop talking politics. She was taken sharply to task in the correspondence columns by Roman Catholics who were appalled by her seeming lack of awareness of the priority the poor have in Roman Catholic proclamation and practice. Few Christians who take the gospel message seriously would disagree with the Church of England's *Faith in the City* report that mutual love and care, and self-sacrificial service to one's neighbour and to one's fellow human beings, lie at the heart of any serious response to the challenge of Jesus.

The considerable achievements of the Church Urban Fund and the continuing and clear commitment of the Church of England not to withdraw from inner city areas has enabled its leaders to speak with integrity about commitment to the poor and disadvantaged. The Archbishop of Canterbury has said:

> The Christian gospel is incorrigibly social and if it stops at the individual it stops! The Christian faith is committed to a just, free and ordered society not because this is a political statement, but because this is God's will for all people. Because we are all made in the image and likeness of God, we are in the business of caring for others.

Squabbles and divisions

To many people on its fringes, the Church seems to spend a lot of time and energy on internal squabbles and divisions which are irrelevant to the rest of the world. There is a good deal of truth in that. The impassioned words of Bishop David Jenkins in the debate on the ordination of women struck a chord with many people when he said: 'Is it not shameful to be quarrelling as we are about women in the Church when the whole world is torn by poverty, strife and lostness?'

The ordination of women to the priesthood has clearly caused problems, but the hope is that the way in which the Church handles its undoubted differences will attract people to faith rather than be a further barrier. There is no doubt that the Church of England's once much vaunted comprehensiveness is currently endangered by a polarisation of the strands within it. This is serious, because a Church which is perceived to be at odds with itself is unlikely to commend itself or its faith.

Many different influences have shaped the Church of England. To Celtic Christianity, Augustine's mission and men such as Anselm, must be added post-Reformation developments such as Puritanism and the Evangelical Revival, as well as the Oxford Movement. There has been a rich tradition of spirituality through people like Julian of Norwich, Lancelot Andrewes, George Herbert, the Wesleys and the Tractarian fathers. The Church of England has an enormously rich inheritance – and it still has the power to speak with great strength to people today.

But what people often see instead is weakness. At the Anglo-Catholic end of the Church, David Hope, Bishop of London, has attacked what he described as the 'negative mind-set of the catholic movement with its seige and ghetto mentality'. Catholics have tended to define themselves by what they are opposed to rather than what they are for. It is said that the Catholic tradition, instead of being seen as what it is – a living thing which is constantly evolving – has come to be treated in the same deadening way that fundamentalist Evangelicals treat the Bible – as if it were a fixed body of teaching which saves you the bother of thinking because it always gives you the same answers, and never says anything new.

Richard Holloway, Bishop of Edinburgh, speaking from the liberal catholic perspective, has warned that there is a strong schismatic energy at work in the Church, and that the drive towards schism, the compulsion to create tidy, homogeneous ecclesiastical units of the usually angry and like-minded, is essentially anti-catholic and sectarian. 'The genius of Catholicism is not sameness, but universality and the generosity that is inclusive, rather than the narrowness of spirit that is always looking for ways of locking people out.' And from the same stable the Bishop of Monmouth, Rowan Williams, has commented:

> We are in a Catholic and a reformed Church; we believe that the real continuity of the gospel is sometimes served by apparent rupture and discontinuity . . . We ought to be able to manage a 'theology of disagreement' – understanding that our diversity is not primarily a mutual threat, but a mutual gift.

There is squabbling too among the Evangelicals who face some possible division with the newly emerged 'Reform' network. A lot of evangelicals want reform but they want the ordination of women too. Will they be able to work with Reform, who are opposed to women's ordination? The key issue for evangelicals in the Church of England will be whether they can maintain their unity.

Then there are the further divisions between the traditional evangelicals and traditional catholics and the liberals. It is unfortunate that 'liberal' has become such a suspect word. Its true meaning was once described as not denoting a creed or a set of philosophical assumptions or any 'ism', but a frame of mind, a quality of character, which it is easier to discern than to define. A liberal-minded person is free from narrow prejudice, generous with judgement on others, and open-minded, especially to the reception of new ideas of proposals for reform. Liberal is the opposite not of conservative, but of fanatical or bigoted or intransigent.

Traditionalist catholics and conservative evangelicals, especially many within the Forward in Faith and Reform movements, accuse the dominant liberal strand of the Church of England of succumbing to the 'spirit of the age'. The reverse may be true. The spirit of this age is increasingly characterised by bigotry, prejudice and self-centredness. It has been described as 'a kind of Alf Garnett mentality that celebrates all that is petty, narrow and parochial'.

Against that dark background, Anglicanism is a beacon of light. It allows people of widely divergent theological stances to belong with integrity to its membership. At its best, it has always sought the mean between two extremes – its very nature is to be middle-of-the-road. This is a strength and not a weakness, and although, at points in its history, the pendulum has swung sometimes in the evangelical and at other times in the catholic direction, its tolerant and comprehensive nature has been for many people its great attraction.

There has been a danger recently of permanent fracture brought about by the tensions of increasingly polarised views. Failure to hold together in the Church of England, and other provinces, and restore firmly within its workings the British virtue of mutual tolerance, will so undermine Anglican credibility that a further barrier to belief will be erected in the minds of those who cannot understand how Christians who are supposed to love one another can behave in such an unloving way.

Disunity among the Churches

The same is true of relationships between the denominations. The Church of England's recent record in ecumenical relations is mixed. At a local level many good things have happened – such as in the case of Liverpool, where relationships between the Churches have been transformed at all levels. But the

Church of England has a habit of encouraging courtship and then jilting its proposed partner when the relationship gets too close.

In the space of one hundred years, not only has the Church of England turned down reunion with the Salvation Army, the Methodists, and the Covenant with the Free Churches, but also, by its vote on the ordination of women to the priesthood, has placed a further serious barrier along the tortuous road to Anglican-Roman Catholic reunion. Hopes for organic unity seem to have faded, and the communion for which Our Lord prayed sometimes seem as far off as ever. It is said that the Church offers to the world a fragmented and flawed facade which does little to help people up the steps of faith.

Certainly the British press has devoted many column inches to point-scoring between the Anglican and Roman Catholic Churches, which hardly endears serious enquirers to the Christian Church. Cardinal Hume's ill-advised remark about the 'conversion of England' was matched by triumphalist remarks from others. These seemed far removed from the earlier assurances of Bishop Cormac Murphy O'Connor that, as far as the Roman Catholic Church is concerned, ecumenism is no longer about 'you-come-in-ism'!

There is little doubt that the disunity of Christians is a major barrier for people who want to explore the Christian faith seriously. Not surprisingly, some feel there must be something deficient about a faith which drives people apart and makes them so intolerant of each other.

But there are positive points too. In 1993 the Porvoo Common Statement between the Anglican and Lutheran Churches signalled the most significant development this century in the move to unity between the European Churches.

In the same year, and therefore since the vote on the ordination of women to the priesthood, the General Synod has been addressed by His All Holiness Patriarch Bartholomew I, the Ecumenical Patriarch and first among equals among the Patriarchs of the Orthodox world. Recognising the great obstacle

which the priesthood of women has put in the path of ecumenism, he said:

> ... we were not discouraged nor did we halt the dialogue,
> since discouragement has no place in the lives of responsible
> persons of faith. Also we recognise that there is not a more
> appropriate and more successful way to resolve differences
> and to grow in the Lord than through the divine gift of the
> dialogue of love and truth.

In the end, the growing together of the divided Christian family
depends on the spirituality of its members. Thomas Merton, the
contemplative Trappist monk, once said that if he could unite
in himself the thought and devotion of Eastern and Western
Christendom, the Greek and Latin fathers, the Russians with
the Spanish mystics, then he could prepare in himself the
reunion of divided Christians. If we want to bring together what
is divided, we cannot do so by imposing one division upon the
other or absorbing one division into the other. If we do this
the union is not Christian, it is political and is doomed to further
conflict. 'We must contain all divided worlds in ourselves and
transcend them in Christ.'

Irrelevant

The Church is far less irrelevant than people sometimes pre-
tend. Boring though much of its worship is perceived to be, it is
certainly not dead. The demise of the Church of England has
long been predicted. In 1558, it seemed to have ended almost
before it had begun, but soon there came the Elizabethan settle-
ment, the age of Jewel and Hooker, and the Caroline years. In
1659, the Book of Common Prayer was forbidden even for private devotion, and faithful clergy were deprived. But within
months there came the re-establishment of the Church and
the Prayer Book of 1662. In 1747 Bishop Butler declined the

Archbishopric of Canterbury on the grounds that 'it is too late to try to save a failing Church'.

In 1832 Thomas Arnold said: 'The Church as it now stands no human power can save.' But in the next year began the Oxford Movement, which brought new life to the Church. In 1880 Bishop Ryle of Liverpool warned: 'The Church of England today is in a more critical and perilous position than at any period in the last two centuries. We are in rough waters, and whether or not we will weather the storm remains to be seen.'

A further hundred years has not changed the message! According to much press coverage, the Church of England is in a spiral of unstoppable decline – a lie which needs to be challenged because misinformation is an unreasonable barrier to place in the path of those who wonder if the Church's message is, after all, true. Accurate figures of church attendance have been kept over many years. The facts show that three decades of Anglican decline stopped in 1987. Since then, overall numbers have been constant. The fact that churches are maintaining their numbers must mean that there are clear areas of growth to offset deaths. Furthermore, during the early 1990s there has been an increase in the numbers of those being confirmed and more people have joined the electoral rolls of parish churches. That does not suggest a church that is irrelevant nor a liturgy that is boring.

With at least six times as many people in church on Sunday as there are at football matches on Saturday, and at a time when voluntary organisations have suffered sharp decline, the Church retains a very firm place within the nation's life. There is far more goodwill for the Church of England, and far more active support for it, than the media leads us to suppose.

Bishop Richard Harries of Oxford pointed out in *The Daily Telegraph*: 'The Tory party, despite all its power of political patronage, could scarcely raise £3m from its members last year. The Diocese of Oxford alone raises £7m from the pews.'

In 1998 the Church of England, as the Mother Church of the Anglican Communion, will be host to more than 800 Bishops at the Lambeth Conference. The Church of England cannot be

understood unless it is seen within this wider context. There are
70 million members of the Anglican Communion. The English-
ness which once was its all embracing mark has long-since
disappeared. Japanese, Korean, Spanish and Brazilian Anglican
bishops will be at Lambeth. The Communion is held together by
affection and common loyalty. Today it has more members and
greater influence in the world than ever before.

The Church of England – and indeed the Anglican Communion – is uniquely placed within the Christian family to
affirm those with doubts and, by its sympathy and understanding, help to remove barriers to belief. On his visit to Papua New
Guinea, the Archbishop of Canterbury visited a cathedral that
had a roof but no walls. People were able to wander in or stay
on the edge – free to listen or go away as they pleased. Using
that as an illustration, he said: 'I believe with all my heart that
the Church of Jesus Christ should be a Church of blurred
edges . . . a Church of no walls where people can ask their hard-
est questions without condemnation and share their deepest
fear without reproach.'

Exclusivism

The Church of England in particular is sometimes under attack
for its perceived exclusiveness. But the fact is that every citizen
belongs to a parish and has a right to be baptised, married and
buried in it. That is about as Christian and unexclusive a system
as can be! Furthermore, other denominations and religions look
to the Church of England as the trustee of all religious faith in
this country. Nevertheless, it is clear that the Church of
England's role in relation to the whole country, which has not
been examined since 1970, needs to be looked at again.

The relationships with ethnic minorities and other faith communities in England; the experience of the rest of the Anglican
Communion, not least that of the Church of Scotland, and the
developing links with other Christian denominations all need
further examination. The role of the senior bishops in the House

of Lords, the Ecclesiastical Committee, and the place of Parliament in Church affairs also require a fresh look – as does the relationship between the Church of England and the Crown.

The Church must not go on the defensive in these matters. People who gingerly approach the steps of faith are more quickly confused than most Anglicans realise by the fact that Parliament controls Church of England legislation and the Prime Minister has the final say in choosing diocesan bishops. And, unwelcome though his comments are in many Anglican quarters, Archdeacon George Austin probably spoke the thoughts of many in raising questions about Prince Charles and the role of the monarch as head of the Church.

I have no doubt at all that it is time to look at these complex matters again, and that reform is not only desirable but long overdue. In my view it is only reform and not wholesale disestablishment that is required.

The Archbishop of York wrote in *The Times* that disestablishment would rightly be seen as signifying that the nation was formally repudiating the Christian heritage and was no longer prepared to pay even lip service to those Christian beliefs and values on which so much of its history and the best of its life have been based. He emphasised that there are millions who still instinctively regard the Church of England as their Church, and look to it not only for weddings, funerals, or baptisms, but at times of stress or trouble or thanksgiving in their lives.

Furthermore, as he pointed out (and I know well from my own links with other denominations and faiths), for the most part members of other Christian Churches, and indeed of the other faiths now present in this country, are not in favour of disestablishment. On the contrary, to a degree which is not widely understood, their leaders often see the fact of establishment as enabling the Church of England to be in the vanguard of action with them, or on their behalf, in matters of common concern.

This was backed up firmly in *The Tablet* by Dr Eamon Duffy, who pointed out that a century ago Cardinal Newman described the established Church as 'a great bulwark against infidelity', and, Dr Duffy added, it remains so. The Church of England maintains a vital Christian presence, not least in the inner cities. Because of the existence of the Church of England, despite the solvents of secularism, Christian values retain a greater hold in Britain's common life than they would otherwise do. As he rightly put it:

> If the Church of England were to be simply dislodged, it would not be in favour of Catholic priests or Methodist ministers or Jewish rabbis. It would be in favour of nothing, the relegation of religion to the realm of the private, and the emptying of our common life of some of the values and assumptions which have shaped it for a thousand years. All would be the losers.

FOR REFLECTION

1 'You don't have to go to church to be a Christian.' Is that true?
2 A Church at odds with itself is unlikely to commend itself or its faith – but the way differences are handled can attract people. How?
3 The teaching of the Church of England is sometimes said, to be woolly. In an age of polarisation and prejudice, is the Church of England's tolerant and middle-of-the-road way a strength or a weakness?
4 How important is unity between the Churches?
5 The Church is dead and boring. Is it?
6 What should be the role of the Church of England in this country?

5

Faiths, Christ and Cults

In our increasingly pluralist society, there is confusion about the relationship between Christianity and other faiths.

When so many wars have religious disputes at their roots, it makes sense for all faiths to work together to enable the world to be at peace. The Roman Catholic theologian, Hans Kung, struck a chord with many when he warned the world's religious leaders that there will be no peace among the nations unless there is peace among the religions.

There are, of course, things in common among the faiths – not least in areas of spirituality – and there are increasing pleas for a global ethic, drawing on the resources of all religions, which would provide a new moral foundation for the world. But that does not mean having a uniform religion or watering down the teachings of other religions. Indeed, respect for the spirituality and belief of other faiths is not achieved by blurring the edges of one's own faith.

The problem for the Christian is, how is it possible to build up respect and understanding of other faiths and co-operate in spirituality and ethics, while at the same time insisting that Christianity alone is the full revelation of God, and continuing to receive converts from other religions? Is it possible simultaneously to honour the other religions and yet put them in second place in a 'league table' of faiths? What about Peter's sermon in which he clearly said about Jesus: 'There is salvation in no-one else, for there is no other name under heaven given among men by which we must be saved'?

All four gospels end with the command to go out, put most explicitly in Matthew's Great Commission: 'Go into all the

world and preach the good news to everyone.' Jesus is quoted by
John as saying: 'I am the way, the truth and the life. No man
comes to the Father except through me.' As the hymn puts it:

> Thou art the way: by Thee alone
> From sin and death we flee
> And he who would the Father seek
> Must seek him Lord by thee.

How then can a way be found for the Christian to acknowledge that truth while at the same time acknowledging that
there are profound truths contained in other faiths? Bernard
Levin, writing in *The Times*, said: 'Many a devout Christian is
worried by this, and many a bishop opening his heart to other
faiths must be hard put to provide an answer. I doubt if you will
get a very convincing answer anywhere, bishop or no bishop!'

Understanding and co-operating

An Indian Christian priest told me of his sorrow that most
Christians do not take seriously the spiritual journeys of those
who follow other routes of faith. In his view we do all worship
the One God, though our interpretations of him may be very
different. The Hindu, the Muslim, the Buddhist, the Sikh are all
on a journey with us to the Father. He pointed out that there
are Hindu temples which have statues of Christ and where the
reading of Christian scriptures is encouraged. They take what
they consider to be the best of Christianity into their own
system.

It is certainly the case that some Christians have become
better Christians because of an insight they have learned from
another faith. My own ordination retreat was taken by a man
who had spent over twenty years as a Christian living in an
Indian ashram imbibing the spirit of contemplation, calmness
and patience. Many of his words and his silences live with me to

this day. The Christian Church has always believed that God has made himself known at many times and in many places.

Fr Bede Griffiths, who until his recent death lived in an Indian ashram, was well known for his commitment to marrying the spiritual strengths of East and West. Mass was celebrated according to the Syrian Christian rite. Readings and prayers were drawn from all the great religions of the world. The external symbols of worship, such as the temple's ornaments and symbols, were Indian. Drawing hundreds of pilgrims each year, that ashram remains a centre for dialogue between religions. It was there that Bede Griffiths developed his basic message: the need to perceive the unity underlying all religions, all creation, and, particularly in the West, the need to recover the sense of the sacred.

The New Testament indicates that God has never left himself without a witness – and that he has spoken to the human race through many inspired people. But in speaking through Jesus he ratified what others had said, and completed and brought to fulfilment all that had gone before. Christianity does not destroy other faiths but completes them. It is not necessary as a Christian to believe that all the other religions are wrong.

C S Lewis said that when he was an atheist he had to try to persuade himself that most of the human race were wrong about the question that mattered to them most. When he became a Christian he was able to take a more liberal view! Remember that in arithmetic, there is only one right answer to the sum; all other answers are wrong. But some of the wrong answers are much nearer being right than others. It is not that Christianity is the only way to God. It is that only by following the way of Christ will we see God as he really is, and truly know him. Thomas Merton put it like this: 'I have found Christ whose centre is everywhere but whose circumference is nowhere.'

The relationship of Christianity to other religions was defined in Roman Catholic terms at the Second Vatican Council in 1966. The Council did not cease to put the Christian faith as the measure of religious truth, but it did say: 'The Catholic Church rejects nothing which is true and holy in these religions.' The

Council notes that, for example, in Hinduism men probe the mystery of God and express it with a rich fund of myths and a penetrating philosophy, and adds that the Church also regards with esteem the Muslims who worship the one, subsistent, merciful and almighty God. Furthermore, 'given the great spiritual heritage common to Christians and Jews, it is the wish of this sacred Council to foster and recommend a mutual knowledge and esteem.'

Within the Anglican tradition, Archbishop William Temple wrote in his famous *Readings in St John's Gospel*: 'There is only one Divine Light and every man in his measure is enlightened by it.' In other words, although he did not view all religions as being equal he did see religious truth as being present in the great teachers such as Isaiah, Plato, Buddha and Confucius.

It follows then that without compromising Christian truth, there is much to be gained from mutual understanding and co-operation with other faiths. That applies not only in spirituality and ethics but, very importantly, in education and community relations – and not least among the younger generations.

In schools, for example, new syllabuses are being introduced which provide children from seven to sixteen with a graded understanding of the six main religions: Christianity, Judaism, Islam, Hinduism, Sikhism and Buddhism. Such an approach is valuable because it encourages an understanding of other religions – though, of course, it does not necessarily help the individual up the steps of personal faith and commitment. It is sometimes wryly said that all the study of comparative religion does is to make people comparatively religious!

Another area of co-operation is over parliamentary issues. The opposition to Sunday trading, for example, came not just from Christian Churches but from the Chief Rabbi too. In the continuing debates on genetic research, Christians, Jews and Muslims have been united, implicitly and explicitly, in condemning a low view of embryonic life. And Anglican bishops, in the House of Lords and also at diocesan level, find themselves acting on behalf of other faith communities, such as on the Asylum Bill and other immigration issues.

But it is important, in attempting to be co-operative, not to misjudge the situation. The Guides Association, in an attempt to encourage ethnic minorities to join them, has removed the pledge 'to do duty to God', and replaced it with a promise 'to do my best to love my God'. The problem there is that the phrase 'my God' may mean anything or nothing! 'My God' could be a pop star, a boyfriend, an all-absorbing pastime, a single-issue commitment (a 'green' world for example) or to the God of heaven and earth. But it is only the last – the God of heaven and earth – which is likely to accord with the faith of Jewish, Muslim, Hindu or Sikh young people. So why 'my God'? Why not simply 'God'? We all agree there is only one God, even though we may describe that God in very different ways. Dr Christopher Lamb, the Church of England's Inter-Faith Relations Secretary, explained that even Hinduism is only an apparent exception here. Buddhists, of course, are non-theists, but even for them 'my God' is no better than 'God'. 'Extensive soundings obviously were taken throughout the Guide movement but it is unlikely that the leading representatives of the other religious traditions would have encouraged the change!'

The Religions of the Book – Islam

As one of the three 'Religions of the Book' Muslims base their faith within the Old Testament – sharing that much with Jews and Christians. In Arabic, the word 'islam' means 'submission to God' and the word 'muslim' means 'one who lives his life according to God's will'. It is a religion of submission and its followers commit themselves to surrender to the will of Allah (God). Especially in its growing fundamentalist forms, it is a stridently missionary religion which emphasises success. It believes that its faith meets all the spiritual and religious needs of mankind.

Islam traces its origin to the Prophet Muhammad who was born in the city of Mecca around AD 571. Married, with three daughters, he began in his middle years to be contemplative and received a revelation to preach the existence of one God. In AD 622 he left Mecca for Medina, and this is the event from which the Muslim calendar begins. In AD 630 he attacked Mecca and rededicated the ancient shrine of the Ka'aba to Allah. It remains the central shrine of pilgrimage for Muslims. Soon after his death in AD 632 his revelations were put together to form the Holy Qur'an. Muslims believe this is the infallible word of God and that nothing has changed it. Simply to recite it brings grace.

According to the Qur'an, Jesus was born of Mary but did not die. Instead, someone died in his place and God raised Jesus to himself. The point there is that death would have been a failure and, in Muslim eyes, a prophet cannot be allowed to fail. To believe that Jesus was God would be the great sin of ascribing partners to God. The idea of God suffering on a cross is totally anathema to all Islamic thought.

For the Muslims there is meant to be no distinction between the personal and communal, the religious and secular, the sacred and profane, or the spiritual and material. They observe the five pillars of Islam:
First, the confession of faith. There is no God but God, and Muhammad is the Prophet of God. Second, prayer. Muslims pray five times daily – at daybreak, noon, mid-afternoon, after sunset, and early in the night. Each is preceded by an obligatory ritual washing and all Muslims face towards Mecca praying as a worldwide single body. Third, fasting (Ramadan). During this month Muslims must not eat or drink, smoke or have sexual relations between dawn and sunset. Fourth, almsgiving. Muslims must give $2\frac{1}{2}\%$ of their income and certain kinds of property to charity. Fifth, pilgrimage. A Muslim is required to go to Mecca once in his lifetime.

Islam and Christianity share many common values: respect for knowledge, concern for justice, compassion for the poor and underprivileged, the importance of family life and respect for parents. But there are times when the differences are obvious. Christmas, for example, can be a very difficult time for many Muslim children. Furthermore, attempts to develop relations between Muslim and Christian leaders can be strained by the fact that in an area where there are several mosques it is often difficult to find a representative leader, because of the autonomy of each mosque.

It is impossible to ignore the worldwide rise of militant fundamentalism in Islam. As Bernard Levin wrote in *The Times*: 'Why has one of the world's most beautiful and profound religions, Islam, been turned into a monstrous charnel house of fanaticism?' But, thankfully, many mosques in this country have moderate leaders. Indeed, as I know from my experience in West Yorkshire, Muslims frequently play an important and positive role – joining other Church leaders in promoting good relations between the communities and also respect for each other's faiths.

Judaism

The film *Schindler's List* has reminded the world, as it needs to be reminded again and again, of the Holocaust and the annihilation of six million Jews. The Jews claim to be the children of Abraham, who around 1800 BC journeyed to Canaan, the promised land. During a time of famine, the twelve sons of Jacob went to Egypt, where they became slaves. In about 1250 BC their descendants were led out by Moses – the Exodus. On the way God made a covenant with Israel enshrined in the Ten Commandments of the Old Testament. The Law, and obedience to it, is central to Judaism. When he is thirteen-years-old a Jewish boy becomes Bar Mitzvah – 'a son of the commandment'.

A devout Jew prays three times a day either at home or in the synagogue – morning, afternoon and evening, covering his head with a hat or skull cap. The centre of Jewish religious life is the home. On a Friday evening, the start of the Sabbath, the woman of the house kindles the sabbath lights. As she does so, she prays for God's blessing on her work and family. The sabbath table is prepared with a clean cloth and laid with two loaves and a cup of wine. Before the evening meal, the husband chants the praise of a virtuous wife and recites verses from the Bible about creation and the Sabbath rest. He then takes the cup of wine and blesses it in the name of God. He also blesses the bread, taking his portion of wine and bread before handing them round.

By traditional indicators, such as synagogue attendance, Anglo-Jewry is in decline. Up to 40% of British Jews marry non-Jews and the number is rising. Rabbi Jonathan Romain has issued a guide for those in mixed-faith relationships which is honest about the difficulties but positive about the solutions. His check list is an invaluable guide for the survival of all mixed faith marriages.

1. Have I discussed fully my religious background, beliefs and customs with my partner?
2. Have I explained properly my view of the relationship to my family – and given my partner a chance to express similar feelings?
3. Have I explained properly my view of the relationship to my partner's family (and listened to my partner's family)?
4. What will happen on our wedding day?
5. What home ceremonies will we have?
6. In what synagogue and other communal activities will we take part?
7. What will happen on festivals with our respective families?
8. How will I fit in with my partner's religious beliefs and practices?
9. What are we going to do about the religious identity of any children?
10. What are we going to do about the religious education of any children?
11. What initiation ceremonies will we have for them?
12. What funeral arrangements do we want?

Such pastoral sensitivity on the part of Jews to non-Jews is a long way from the attitude of Christians to Jews in, for example, the words of Pius X in 1904: 'The Jews have not recognised our Lord; therefore we can not recognise the Jewish people.' Pope John XXIII went on to make the declaration that the Jews were 'a perfidious race'. But in 1986 Pope John Paul II paid a visit to the Rome synagogue and spoke of Jews as Christianity's beloved elder brothers. Understandably, Jews continue to regard many Christians with deep suspicion, and not least because of the present Decade of Evangelism.

The Lambeth Conference of 1988 stated in Appendix 6 on Jews, Christians and Muslims:

> There are those Christians whose prayer is that Jews, without giving up their Jewishness, will find their fulfilment in Jesus the Messiah. Indeed some regard it as their particular vocation and responsibility to share their faith with Jews, whilst at the same time urging them to discover the spiritual riches which God has given them through the Jewish faith . . . All these approaches . . . share a common concern to be sensitive to Judaism.

Christ – uniqueness or particularity?

So how is Christianity to cope with the crucial issue of its relationship to other faiths? The belief that God is one belongs to several faiths. What is unique in the Christian understanding of God is that, through Christ, he is shown to be a God of love and forgiveness. He cares above all for the lost and the outcast, for the sick and the suffering. But, does such a God confine himself to one religion? Is there really convincing proof of the superiority of Christianity over other religions in the fields of saintliness, spirituality or social organisation?

Professor John Hick says that Christianity must now abandon the claim that Jesus was the unique Son of God. Christianity should be understood as one among many different human responses to 'the ultimate transcendence Reality that we call God'. In order to foster world peace and a common ethic he argues for major departures from previously cherished positions. For example, Christians would need to look in a new way at the Trinity, Muslims would need to consider revision of the medieval sharia law, and Jews would have to discover forgiveness and renunciation, beginning with the Holocaust.

Oxford's Regius Professor of Divinity, Keith Ward, goes further. Religion, he now claims, is out of date and should give way to 'an age of convergent spirituality'. He argues that Christians will have to abandon the Virgin Birth, the physical Resurrection and the notion that Jesus is in any literal sense unique.

Professor Maurice Wiles argues that Christian exclusivism contradicts the Christian concept that God loves all people. Exclusivism means that salvation can come only through faith in Christ. As we have noted, this is increasingly felt within many Christian circles to be arrogant. Inclusivism means that God has revealed himself supremely in Christ, but that he is also bringing people to salvation who do not know Christ and who may belong to other faiths. This viewpoint is growing in popularity. Pluralism means that salvation can come through all religions – because they lead to God through different cultures and histories, and faith in Christ is only one way among many. This is a very popular viewpoint, but in my view it is wrong.

The distinctively Christian contribution in relation to all this is to say that God is Christ-like. The Christ-likeness of God is found in his forbearance, longsuffering nature, his love and charity – and in the bearing of the pain of the cross. God is Christ-like in his tolerance. Christians also are called to be Christ-like and to exhibit those same qualities – and indeed bear something of the pain. The Archbishop of Canterbury has said that it is the pain of believers to learn that 'to tolerate' is not just the right thing to do, but the moral and just way to be. The genuinely tolerant are not those who are indifferent to others who believe different things. They are the ones who, themselves of passionate beliefs, are able also to enter the pain which others feel.

In *The Independent*, the Archbishop spoke of the shame of the Christian Church in fostering anti-semitism: 'I reject all those forms of faith which coerce others and which in so doing reduce the Christian faith to being a weapon. Augustine long ago took the words of the parable "compel them to come in" as a command to force people to obey. That was wrong and will remain wrong.'

Many Christians who get upset by what they think is a weakening of the Christian line in relation to other faiths have probably never engaged in serious conversation with people of different religions. It is preferable to begin our thinking with Hindu and Muslim people, rather than with Hinduism and Islam. It is also important to use words like 'unique' very carefully. Is the 'uniqueness of Christ' in fact an appropriate phrase for a Christian to use? The truth is that we are all unique!

I have found Bishop David Silk especially helpful in this. Noting St Paul's words that 'God was in Christ reconciling the word to himself' he prefers to speak not of the uniqueness of Jesus but of his 'particularity'. Salvation was and is focused through him. He is the criterion by which are to be judged all understandings of divinity and salvation.

But to say Christ is unique is to go a step too far, for there is no warrant for it in scripture. It is claiming that God's pattern of salvation is found in its fullness in Christ, and that it is not found in any significant way in any other. 'But', says Bishop Silk, 'who am I to say that? I am a Christian, a disciple of the one who warned us against sitting in judgement over others.'

It is the experience of many Christians – and I include myself in this – that we can also glimpse God and recognise goodness, holiness and love in people who are nourished by other religious traditions. It is a paradox and we do not know quite how to explain it. But as Bishop Silk said: 'All we do know is that we must bear witness to the truth as we have received it, and yet acknowledge that God has not left himself without witness outside our tradition.'

Cults

Writing in *The Times*, William Rees-Mogg described letters he had received from people who had had valuable religious experiences, which would be regarded as wholly normal in Eastern cultures. Instead, here in the West, they find that they are prescribed tranquillisers if they mention such experiences even to their families, and that the clergy themselves are embarrassed by them.

This suspicion of religious experience has led to a vacuum being created. It has been said that the Church must re-emerge from the cul-de-sac of rationalism and secularisation, which acts as a barrier for many people's search for faith, and take seriously the search for spirituality which, for example, the New Age movement represents.

Unfortunately, this spiritual vacuum has led to the rise of more than five hundred cults now said to be operating in the United Kingdom. These are new religious movements, usually falling into one of the two categories: cults masquerading as religious orders, which tend to attract younger people in their early twenties, and those which offer some sort of therapeutic help for physical or mental problems and which are more popular with people in their mid-thirties or older. There are also an increasing number of cults which present themselves as management or assertiveness training groups. Their often manipulative methods are far removed from the open and unthreatening styles of evangelism which the main religions in this country are now trying to establish.

Mind control techniques used in cults include meditation, 'love-bombing' (when recruits are hugged and kissed and shown a great deal of affection by members), chanting and singing, sleep and food deprivation, and fatigue. Unlike earlier movements – such as Jehovah's Witnesses and Mormons – many of these cults have emerged from traditions that are still alien to most Westerners. Although there may *seem* to be some common features between the movements, the fact is that there are enormous differences between them in every area of belief and practice.

What is reassuring is that the vast majority of those who become involved suffer no permanent serious damage as a result of their involvement. A small minority, however, do. Dr Eileen Barker, in a study sponsored by the Home Office, has identified the following as potentially dangerous situations: a movement cutting itself off (either geographically or socially) from the rest of society; a convert becoming increasingly dependent on the movement for definitions and the testing of 'reality'; a movement drawing sharp, non-negotiable boundaries between 'them' and 'us', 'godly' and 'satanic', 'good' and 'bad', etc; important decisions about converts' lives being made for them by others; leaders claiming divine authority for their actions and their demands; leaders or movements pursuing a single goal in a single-minded manner.

One of the most tragic incidents recently has been the Waco holocaust. Much criticism has been made of the failure of the media and authorities to understand the cult's beliefs. For example the BBC's *Newsnight* presenter cut short an explanation of the theological basis of the beliefs of the cult's leader, David Koresh. Professor David Martin observed that this was typical of the predominantly secular view that belief systems were not the significant factor at Waco. To the uninformed secular mind, of course, it all seems bizarre – but in fact Koresh had a thoroughly standard belief system. What he did that was extreme was to detach this group of followers and take them through a period of sustained social isolation.

Writing in *The Daily Telegraph* about the Waco tragedy, Bishop Tom Butler of Leicester commented on the sad truth that mystical insight and mad illusion seem to lie close together in the human psyche. As he pointed out, the great religions have always known this, and so they have their checks and balances through worship, prayer and pastoral care. Ordinary worshippers can get in touch with the reality of God without destroying themselves in the process. But when people are drawn into a pseudo-religious movement such as at Waco, then they become incapable of seeing reason, because they are too busy seeing visions.

The Bishop observed that the psychological danger posed in these cases is obvious, but that there is an equally real theological danger: 'I believe that the lust for certainty is the original human sin.' A religious or political leader offering the fruit of certainty will always have followers, who will sometimes follow him or her to their deaths. 'I am disturbed by those who have terrible doubts about religion, but I am even more disturbed by those who have terrible certainties.'

Looking at reasons why people are attracted to cults, Bishop Tom Butler noted that it is precisely because the local church does not provide confident leadership in teaching a resilient faith that people fall into the hands of dogmatic sectarian charlatans; and it is because the local church does not provide a welcoming community and uplifting spirituality that people are vulnerable to love-bombing and intoxicating worship. Bishop Tom Butler concludes:

> It need not be so. There are many local churches where good open leadership is to be found, which offer sound teaching within the context of an attractive community and uplifting worship. The aim of such churches is to enable people to broaden and deepen their faith through a process of thoughtful holiness, and to do this, not by withdrawing from a wicked world but by touching a wounded world with some of the grace of God. I wish there were more churches like this.

FOR REFLECTION

1   In what way is Christianity different from other faiths?
2   In what ways can the different religions and faith communities co-operate?
3   Is it correct to speak of the uniqueness of Christ?
4   All the study of comparative religions does is to make

people comparatively religious! Is it important for children to know the beliefs and ways of other faiths?

5   Why are people attracted to cults?

6

Suffering, God and Unanswered Prayer

Children killed – why?

At the end of November 1993, twelve children and their teacher, nearing home after a happy visit to a concert at the Albert Hall in London, were killed in an accident on the M40. *The Sunday Telegraph* put the question bluntly: 'How can you believe in a loving, all powerful God who allows such tragedy to happen?' For many people this is the biggest barrier to faith.

In the days following the accident, several attempts were made in newspaper articles and letters by Christian leaders to give a response to the question 'why?' One answered plainly that we do not know why there should be a God who lets these awful things happen. We live in a world of real values: positive and negative. If the universe was just made up of electrons, then there would be no problem of suffering, or indeed of evil. Tragedies such as this need not call into question belief in God. Rather they prevent any kind of settling into a cosy ideal of God as pushy and controlling. Christians believe in a crucified, victim God who is on the receiving end of pain and evil.

Another observed that when these public tragedies happen, our largely godless society calls in trauma experts and counsellors – and then presumes to question why God did nothing about the tragedy. He protested that you really cannot treat religion as just one option among many consumer lifestyles, and then suddenly start slinging profound religious questions at God – in whom, until three days ago, you had no particular religious belief! Noting that the problem of innocent suffering was a question Job put before God, he likewise concluded that the question is unanswerable.

God did in fact answer Job in his apparently pointless suffering. It was with a riddle – but nevertheless Job was comforted. There may be many explanations of why a tragedy happens, but we will never know the answer to the deepest question of why God allowed it to take place until the day when all things are known.

It is, of course, entirely proper at a time of tragedy to doubt God's goodness and to question the meaning of what has happened. But God has not made an accident-free universe. To do so would rob us of a real freedom of choice in our actions. One leader pointed out that the Christian faith does not offer a philosophical explanation of such disasters, but a way of coping with them. The crucifixion of Jesus shows that God does not stand aloof from our sufferings but shares them and helps us work through them to a new beginning.

The only thing which people who have faith can hold on to is the fact that God loves us so much that he will choose exactly the right moment to call us back to him. For the parents and the family of the driver, said one priest, the comfort they could draw on was that God knows when this right time is. 'I cannot think of a more profound theological point than that. The grief is purely on our part. There is rejoicing in heaven at the thought of angels joining the throngs.'

Someone then took up the point that God failed to protect the children. Such a view, he emphasised, was against Christian thought. Religion has never been an insurance policy. God has created a free world in which tragedy may happen and he suffers as much as we do. If God were to step in crudely and arbitrarily it would pose more questions than it would solve. Why should he protect twelve Christian children and ignore ten thousand Hindus dying in an earthquake?

Then there was the comment that the pain of the human condition has always been agonising, that it is impossible to believe in God because of the blackness and agony in the universe. And it is impossible *not* to believe in God because of the beauty and the glory in it. Faith tilts the balance towards one impossibility. The Christian sees a window into the mystery in the crucifixion of the Lord on Calvary.

A very different viewpoint, which also gained much coverage, was put by Richard Dawkins. The universe, he said, is in fact ruled by blind indifference. He poured scorn on such attempts to respond to the 'so-called' problem of suffering. Writing shortly after the tragedy of the deaths of the children, he referred to the answer given by one of the Church leaders that, if the universe were just electrons, there would be no problem of evil or suffering. It was hard to imagine a more vacuously unconvincing chain of reasoning. If the universe were indeed just 'electrons' and selfish genes, meaningless tragedies like the crashing of the bus are exactly what we should expect, along with equally meaningless good fortune. 'Such a universe would be neither bad nor good in intention. It would manifest no intentions of any kind.' He argued that in a universe of physical forces and genetic replication, some people are going to get hurt, other people are going to get lucky, and there will be no rhyme or reason in it, nor any justice. 'The universe that we observe has precisely the properties we should expect if there is, at bottom, no design, no purpose, no evil and no good, nothing but blind, pitiless indifference.'

The problem that the Christian faces in responding to people like Dr Dawkins is that, as we have already noted, there is, and never has been, an answer to the problem of suffering. Indeed there is, as some would perceive it, a helplessness about God which is embarrassing. That is not new. St Mark recording in his Gospel the visit that Jesus made to his home town writes: 'He could do no mighty works there.' (Mark 6:5) But St Matthew, writing probably a decade later, and using Mark's account, changes it to: 'He did not do many mighty works there, because of their unbelief.' (Mark 13:58) For Mark it was clear that Jesus was unable to act. But Matthew changes the verb because he cannot bear the thought of Jesus being thwarted. It was not that he could not; he did not.

We may feel the same tension in facing tragedy. Surely if God really is God, he can do anything, whether or not you and I allow him to do so? Or is God actually helpless to prevent tragedy or personal suffering. Doesn't he care? Is it that God's hands are tied by love? He is determined to let us be free, slowly and painfully to grow up, and to make good. If he were to manipulate he would not be love and we would not be human. But one is tempted to ask if our freedom is worth the heavy price of so much suffering.

Then there are the arguments that God chastises and purifies those whom he loves, so that they may serve him better. Well, I have certainly come across people in my pastoral ministry where courage and cheerfulness in the face of great pain and suffering has been a tremendous witness. Without doubt there are those who are given the inner strength to transcend their suffering in a wonderful way.

But I think, too, of the many occasions when the suffering has been a terrible experience for both the sufferer and close friends and relatives. It is all too easy to be pious when discussing these matters. The truth is that, in many of these tragic situations, when the facts of faith meet the unpalatable experiences of life, the result can be brutally devoid of meaning. I remember one young man, ravaged by cancer, with a young wife and children, crying his eyes out and asking again and again: 'What is the point?' And when he eventually and painfully died, his wife cried bitterly: 'Why did he have to suffer like that – and why for so long?'

What can a Christian say in those situations? Words seem so inadequate. There have been times when I have been with suffering people, and I have wanted to cry, and sometimes I have cried. Perhaps that's how God feels about it too. And maybe the unspoken, tearful love that still comes from him is the one thing we are given to convey in these tragic moments. Then, what helps is not what we say, but our tears of love, or simply squeezing a hand or putting our arm round a shoulder.

One day we will understand – but not now – on that day when God calls us home and wipes away all tears from our eyes.

Suffering is part of faith – albeit an unpleasant ingredient. But, as Paul said in Romans 8:18: 'I consider that our present sufferings are not worth comparing with the glory that will be revealed in us.' It is that hope of heaven which puts into context the place of suffering in this life.

Suffering has always been part of the human experience. But it is not, within the whole scheme of things, pointless waste. Natural selection has provided a rationale for waste. There can be no creation without destruction and no life without death. And the God who holds up the creative process is also the one who bears its weight in suffering.

The Suffering God

Is that the nearest we can get to an answer to the question: Where is God when we need him on earth?

Where was God when six million Jews died? One of the survivors of the concentration camps told Rabbi Dan Cohn-Sherbok, writing in *The Times*, that it never occurred to him to question God's doings or lack of doings while he was in inmate of Auschwitz. His faith in God was not undermined in the least. 'It never occurred to me to associate the calamity we were experiencing with God – to blame him or to believe in him less, or cease believing in him at all because he didn't come to our aid.' He added, 'God doesn't owe us that, or anything. We owe our lives to him. If someone believes that God is responsible for the death of six million because he didn't somehow do something to save them, he's got his thinking reversed.'

Jurgen Moltmann, in his book *The Crucified God*, quotes another survivor of Auschwitz describing how the SS hanged two Jewish men and a youth in front of the whole camp. The men died quickly, but it took the youth longer to die. One Jew, forced to watch, asked: 'Where is God? Where is he?' Later on, as the youth still hung in torment in the noose the man called again, 'Where is God now?' 'And I heard a voice in myself answer: Where is he? He is here. He is hanging there on the gallows.'

The idea of a suffering God has a powerful appeal for some in a century of unprecedented horror and brutality. But the Christian teaching of earlier times tended towards the view that God could not suffer. St Ignatius described God as: 'Him who is above all seasons, timeless, invisible, who for our sakes became visible, who cannot be touched, who cannot suffer.' St Anselm, in the eleventh century, asked how God could be at once pitiful and impassible.

But can our twentieth century make sense of the being of God unless he is a God who shares in the world's suffering – a God who understands, and accepts and lovingly transforms that suffering? Writing of the Aberfan tragedy, when a great pile of coal waste slipped, burying and killing children in the school below, W H Vanstone said in his book *Love's Endeavour, Love's Expense*: 'God is not a god who from the top of the mountain caused or permitted it to happen, but a God who received at the foot of the mountain its appalling impact.'

Rabbi Albert Friedlander, in an Easter message for *The Independent*, said that in the days between Passover and Easter, he found himself closer to Christians than at any other time – and also more remote from them. The fact that God accompanies and then suffers with us is not necessarily a consolation, 'but it brings us back to the belief that both traditions must understand the intertwining of humanity and God in the fields of suffering.'

Few people have expressed this more effectively, in ways that ordinary people can understand, than the First World War chaplain, Geoffrey Studdert Kennedy. Known affectionately as 'Woodbine Willie' because of his ready supply of cigarettes for the wounded and dying in the trenches, he tried to cope in simple rhyme with the questions men ask when they come face to face with the horror of war. In his poem 'The Suffering God' he tried to make some sense of all the futility and waste.

> How can it be that God can reign in glory,
> Calmly content with what his love has done,

Reading unmoved the piteous shameful story
All the vile deeds men do beneath the sun?

Are there no tears in the heart of the Eternal?
Is there no pain to pierce the soul of God?
Then must he be a fiend of hell infernal,
Beating the earth to pieces with his rod.

Or is it just that there is nought behind it,
Nothing but forces purposeless and blind?
Is the last thing, if moral men could find it,
Only a power wandering as the wind?

Father, if he the Christ were thy Revealer
Truly the first begotten of the Lord,
Then must thou be a Suff'rer and Healer,
Pierced to the heart by the sorrow of the sword.

Then must it mean, not only that thy sorrow
Smote thee that once upon the lonely tree,
But that today, tonight and on the morrow,
Still it will come, O Gallant God to Thee.

The Christian message is not just that God identifies with suffering. He redeems us from it. The God who suffers is also powerful in resurrection.

Unanswered prayer

For those who pray that people may be spared the tragedy of pain and suffering, seemingly unanswered prayer can be a forbidding barrier to faith. To pour out your heart to what seems to be a dull and unanswered silence is a deeply discouraging and frustrating experience. But the Bible itself is full of unanswered prayers. Moses prayed to enter the Promised Land – but he died on the mountain top with his request refused. The

Psalmist, in words quoted by Jesus on the cross, cried: 'My God, my God, why have you forsaken me? Why are you so far from helping me, and from my words of complaint?' Habakkuk pleaded: 'O Lord, how long shall I cry and you will not hear?' Paul prayed that the thorn in his flesh would leave him – but it did not.

So what did Jesus mean when he said: 'Call me and I will answer . . . Ask and it shall be given to you . . . If you ask anything in my name, I will do it.' Paul wrote in his letter to the Romans: 'We do not know how to pray as we ought'. The truth is that God knows our needs, and he always answers prayers in one of two ways. Either he changes the circumstances or he supplies sufficient power to overcome them. As Mother Julian of Norwich put it long ago: 'He said not: thou shalt not be tempested, thou shalt not be travailed, thou shalt not be afflicted; but he said: thou shalt not be overcome.'

Prayer must never be a substitute for intelligence and hard work. It is not about asking God to do for us what we should be doing ourselves. We ought not to expect a response to our prayers until we have done our best to create the conditions under which our prayer can be answered. If we are ill, or have toothache, or have emotional problems, then, as well as praying, we need to see a doctor, a dentist, or a psychiatrist. And there is no point in praying for spiritual growth unless we do our best to live disciplined Christian lives. And can we honestly pray for social justice and world peace if we do nothing to stop our own greed and selfishness and hate?

In any case, we have to ask ourselves if the things we think we want are in fact what we need. A life without problems would itself be a problem, for when we are removed from suffering we are cut off from joy. An Easter faith which rings true is always a faith which includes the wounds of Calvary.

Donald Nicholl, in his book *Holiness*, said that if we were to ask ourselves what could be the very worst thing that could happen to us in life, the answer would have to be the complete opposite of the answer that worldly folk give:

The worst thing that could happen to me in this life is that I should always have perfect health, always have interesting work and plenty of money to buy things and take holidays, and manage somehow never to be brought into contact with suffering. If that were to happen to me I should be turned into a monster, something unnatural, incapable of compassion for other creatures. To be cut off from suffering is automatically to be cut off from joy. And since man is made for joy, one would have failed monstrously to become what one was meant to be if one were cut off from suffering. Whenever we are removed from suffering for any length of time, therefore, we can be certain that we are on the wrong path.

FOR REFLECTION

1 Does the presence of so much suffering in the world suggest there is no God?
2 What is the Christian response to the question: Why does God allow suffering?
3 Does God suffer?
4 What experience have you had of your prayers being unanswered?
5 What should we pray for?

7

Evil, Moral Values and Sex

Evil

The sheer horror of seeing, on our television screens, Rwandan children macheted to death, and countless bodies floating in rivers and lakes, has been yet another vivid and tragic reminder of man's inhumanity to man and the ever-present existence of evil in our world. No wonder people question how such a world can be governed by a God that is good.

Is it God who is responsible for creating sin and evil? And if so, how does that fit in with what Christians claim to be his loving purposes of saving the world? Is there a divine plan which includes evil? If there is not, and God is not in any way responsible for these terrible things, then does he have any power to help us? How is it possible to have faith in a world like this?

Concluding a fascinating series in *The Independent* on providence and the problem of evil, Professor Paul Helm argued that faith cannot be totally blind, a gamble in the face of infinite odds. Faith, if it is intelligible and defensible, must have some evidence going for it.

We may trust God, in the face of evil, not by an act of blind faith, but because there are other parts of the ways of God that are eminently trustworthy. God has a plan; parts of that plan are intelligible to us, and we trust him for what at present it is hard to make sense of. But does that mean there is little we can do about evil?

Where does the Church stand in all this? Many feel the Christian Church could and should do far more to emphasise goodness and the need for a moral base to life.

The killing of James Bulger hit the nation and induced a deep mode of self-questioning in a manner which few other tragedies have done. 'It was', said the judge, 'an act of unparalleled evil and barbarity.' How did two mentally normal boys aged ten and of average intelligence, come to commit this terrible crime? The boys themselves seem to have had little if any moral sense – as evidenced by what seem to have been lies, sustained cruelty, lack of loyalty to each other, and lack of real remorse. Lord Jakobovits said in *The Times* that the removal of a sense of shame has changed our moral vocabulary, encouraging the unacceptable to become accepted. We look round and see a world in moral chaos.

In this situation is it possible to distinguish between good and evil? In a recent papal encyclical, *Veritatis Splendor*, the Pope answers that last question clearly. There is absolute evil and there is also absolute good. We must distinguish between the two, not merely in others but also in ourselves. That is the meaning of conscience. In contrast to the current view that it is up to each individual to work out a moral code, the encyclical argues that although we have the freedom to decide and act, we cannot invent moral values about such things as individual dignity, honesty and human rights.

It is wrong to judge that an action is right or wrong because of its motive or the consequences of that action. The fact is that some acts are wrong in themselves; they cannot be made right by the motive or intention of the person doing them, or by the consequences that ensue. The encyclical does give human freedom and the individual conscience its proper place. However, it also emphasises that as human beings each one of us has a responsibility and duty to pursue the truth. The truth is not just the product of our own imagination, it is of God and his purpose for us. The Pope's strong emphasis on the Churches' duty to teach that morality applies both to personal and family life and to social and political life is very welcome. We are all capable of both good and evil. Our capacity for evil, pride, greed, lust and envy at all levels needs to be contained – and our innate capacity for good released.

Freedom to choose between good and evil is the essential basis of the moral life. But freedom of choice is not an end in itself. It brings with it duties, and personal and social responsibility, which in turn strengthen the community and deepen human relationships. But freedom must be related to truth. The problem there is: what is truth? We have become so used to impermanence, not least in human relationships, that it is tempting to think that everything is in a state of perpetual flux, that there are no universal and abiding truths about human nature itself, and thus no moral norms which are valid in every age.

Nevertheless, unless it has been totally suppressed, we do have an inner sense of moral obligation. Instinctively we know that good must be done and evil avoided. We also know that all that is needed for evil to triumph is for good men to do nothing. That was part of the problem in the James Bulger murder – as so many witnesses, who saw him being dragged away to his death, and did nothing, now understand all too well. *The Independent* noted, 'Our culture holds busybodies in low esteem, but James's case shows us that indifference is a worse thing.'

We live in a culture that treasures choice and self-expression above everything else. Writing in *The Tablet*, a teacher described a class invited to consider a hypothetical moral dilemma faced by a young woman.

Teacher: 'So what are the choices open to her? What should she do?'

Students: 'It's up to her.'

Teacher: 'Yes. I know it is up to her. But what should she do?'

Students: 'It's her choice.'

Teacher: 'Yes, we know it's her choice. But how should she choose? And on what grounds?'

Students: 'It's her choice.'

A professor from Bradford University wrote in *The Independent*: 'Anyone who teaches undergraduates today will tell you that the most prevalent reactions they have to most social and moral issues is a jejeune selectivism: "It's all a matter of opinion isn't it?" '

Some people are put off the Christian faith because they perceive confusion among Church leaders, a weak moral lead, and a reluctance to teach the difference between right and wrong. That is unfair. Many is the pulpit from which that distinction is taught, and many are the occasions when Christian leaders speak clearly in papers and magazines, on radio and television. There was unhesitating and unanimous agreement, in the wake of the James Bulger tragedy, of the crucial importance of the Churches continuing to do that.

But Cardinal Hume was surely correct in *The Daily Mail* when he pointed out that it is equally crucial for such teaching to be done by parents in the home and teachers at school. Example is far more powerful than words. There can be no substitute for a secure and loving home. No school can make up for the lack of good parents. But love does not mean always giving in to children's demands. They need stability, consistency and discipline. They need clear rules so they learn to channel their energies constructively and develop a sense of right and wrong. Otherwise freedom and liberty become licence.

The family

One of my local members of Parliament in West Yorkshire, Geoffrey Lofthouse, a committed Anglican, has spoken in public of his dismay that there are now more than 1.25 million families without a father. Out of wedlock parenthood, he suggests, correlates with anti-social behaviour, bad neighbourliness, problem children, delinquency, low achievement, fraud and crime – in short with an emergent underclass: 'So I am in no doubt that when the conventional two parent family is threatened, our whole society is put at risk.'

The family is the basic community – the place where the deepest experiences of love, trust, self-acceptance and growth in intimacy can take place, where suffering can be supported and evil contained. It is parents who are the first and principal educators of their children. It is in the family that moral values are inculcated and practised. That is where right and wrong are learned, and where respect for love and life become instilled. In other words, the influence of a parent for good or ill is incalculable.

The reality, as Cardinal Hume has consistently emphasised, is that too many families fail to become those sources of love and stability. It is highly alarming that the institution of the family is being severely undermined. We have reached a situation where to have a healthy family is fundamentally at odds with the present values of our culture because a family, by its nature, is radically anti-individualist.

In a society where the vision of family and community begins to be weakened and the individual is seen to be all-important, people inevitably relate less well together and become more isolated. Then selfishness and lawlessness take over. Taking family responsibilities seriously leads people away from seeing themselves as the centre of their world.

The Archbishop of Canterbury has likewise insisted that children who grow up without proper guidelines, without adequate discipline, without a knowledge of good and evil, right and wrong, are children who are inadequately prepared for life. This is why parenting courses are becoming increasingly important. Far too many children have grown up on a diet of loveless insecurity – and their fragile moral antennae are vandalised beyond repair.

The Chief Rabbi has joined Christian leaders in saying that the habit of self-restraint should be passed on within the family in early childhood to be reinforced later by the education system and the local community. Since the late 1950s our systems of moral transmission have broken down. Not only has the family undergone a spectacular collapse, but, equally alarmingly, the educational system has moved from an ethic of self-restraint to one of self-expression. Communities have disintegrated into societies of strangers. The primary victims have been our children who, without rules and habits to chart them through a complex world, turn to truancy, alcohol, drugs, violence and crime.

The Church

The potential influence of the Churches through the teaching and nurture provided in the Church schools is enormous. The need for them to promote moral and spiritual values has never been stronger. In 1990–91 more than 800,000 pupils attended Church of England primary and secondary schools; 773,00 attended Roman Catholic Schools; and 16,000 were at Methodist schools. Many of these schools were over-subscribed – and therefore higher figures could have been recorded had there been places. The 1992 report on British Social Attitudes makes it clear that a large majority of the population still want to think of themselves as part of a Christian culture.

Speaking in West Yorkshire recently, the Archbishop of Canterbury underlined the fact that the Church does have principles to share with society. He told a famous story by Wittgenstein about a man's attempt to escape from a house. The man tried to window, the chimney – even a panel leading to a secret passage – but all to no avail. He fell into a chair, in total despair, exhausted. Then he noticed that the front door had been open all the time! The point is that we seek difficult ways of getting out when there may be an obvious way before us. So it might seem in the case of morality. The Archbishop went on:

> To those who say: there are no objective standards to guide us any longer, I would point to the Judaeo-Christian emphasis upon the Ten Commandments which have been the fundamental stratum of western morality for centuries. Here is still a framework, a code, which has been tested and tried. The door still remains open for people to enter. Yes, there is a

price to pay; we have to surrender our private, individualised morality and succumb to a standard which will challenge the 'get rich quick' and the 'pleasure bent' culture of our day. For Christians, the teachings of Jesus and the pattern of his life will provide an additional framework for our Christian living. A privatised morality like a privatised religion fails. It is time as a nation we recovered our sense of right and wrong.

Strange then, that after such plain speaking that some have accused the Church of England of being strangely quiet about teaching the difference between right and wrong. It was an accusation made much of by the press when put by a Government Minister, David Maclean. However, the Church of England found an ally in the Cabinet Minister, Peter Lilley, who said: 'It's never reported when the Church is doing good things. The Archbishop of Canterbury has given some very good sermons and lectures on family values. I've read some of them, but they are never reported.'

The Church of England Newspaper published extracts from some of the addresses which the Archbishop of Canterbury had given in the previous year about the spiritual vision for our society, the privatisation of morality, the overriding importance of the family, and the abiding value of the Ten Commandments. He spelt out his message clearly. 'Alongside a renewal of faith, I want to see renewed commitment to the God given principles of good living set out in the Ten Commandments and elaborated in the New Testament.' The newspaper concluded that it is not right to say that the top leadership of the Church of England is silent on matters of right and wrong. Nor, on the whole, are parish clergy, and the many Anglican voluntary societies.

Sex

For many people, the Churches' perceived or real attitudes to sex act as barriers to belief. As Monica Furlong put it in *The Independent*: 'If you are a Christian, then God help you if you are not born in the sexual mould.' She wryly observed that in other areas of Christian obedience you are allowed the odd deviation – wealth for instance, or usury, or fighting, all things rather far from the spirit of Jesus of Nazareth – 'but sexually, my word, you know what you had better not do.'

The point is that the sexual burdens the Churches place on men and women are felt by many to be built on a shameful hypocrisy and a conspiracy of silence. As everyone knows the 'rules' are widely flouted. She regretted that gentle understanding and empathy seem to be less prized in the churches than sexual control and conformity.

Into what is clearly still an area of confusion and uncertainty, the recent statement by the House of Bishops' *Issues in Human Society* has been welcomed by some as a breath of fresh air. At the very least it is a considered and serious response to the problems of sexual activity, and perhaps one of the most sensible and carefully nuanced short surveys of the subject currently available. The document discusses the relevant material in the Bible, the problems posed by modern experience in heterosexual and homophile (the word the Bishops use in preference to homosexual) relationships, as well as sexual discipline within the Church today.

The position which we have adopted as bishops is an essentially conservative one. We affirm chastity before marriage, and fidelity within it, as the ideal. At the same time, we fully recognise that there is no lack of fullness in someone who chooses to remain single and is happily so. We are prepared to extend a welcome within the Church to those who are living in sexually active homophile relationships – and as a parish priest I did so – but we do not, nor did I, commend such a way of life.

The document does address the matter of some forms of sex outside marriage, but is clear in its assertion that full physical sexual relations have no place in the life of the single person. They find their proper fulfilment in the context of a 'unique life long commitment to one partner'.

The nature of the marriage relationship lies at the heart of the matter. When is a marriage not a marriage? If the relationship does not aspire to its high ideals, or for one reason or another has died – then does it cease to be a marriage altogether? And does that free the couple to engage in a loving sexual relationship with someone else? The official teaching is unmistakable in its answer: No. However, Bishop Spong's *Living in Sin?* claims that it is not marriage that makes sex holy, but the nature of the relationship. He argues in favour of the recognition of the state of betrothal, a faithful, committed and public relationship, but one which is not legally binding and is not necessarily for life. In his view, sexual intercourse does not have to be reserved until a contract has been formally entered into.

The House of Bishops' statement considers same-sex relationships and allows that homosexuality may have genetic or psychological origins. There is a common humanity shared by heterosexual and homophile people which is lived, but 'in different ways which makes a distinctive contribution of each essential for the fullness of human kind as a whole'. However, there is a mismatch for homosexual people between their sexuality and their capacity for parenthood, and between their bodies and the ways in which they wish to express their mutual self giving.

As bishops, we are clear that clergy cannot claim the liberty to enter into sexually active homophile relationships. That does not mean that I, or my colleagues, intend to search out and expose clergy who are living in that way – though, clearly, if this adversely affected their public ministry or scandal began to develop, I would intervene firmly. All bishops and most Church members believe that those who are ordained should do their utmost to set an example that will best witness to the Church's teaching on sexuality.

I think we all recognise that there is still more thinking and praying to be done about that teaching. No area is more delicate and sensitive than that of human relationships – with its highly complex interplay between love, commitment and sexual intercourse. The distinction between what is right and wrong in sexual relationships is far less obvious than some fundamentalist Christians would like to claim. Indeed, it disturbs me deeply

when those who trumpet the love of Jesus collude with the spirit
of the age in viewing sexual misdemeanour as a greater sin
than the obscenity, for example, of starving children. I do not
condone sexual misdemeanour at all – but there is something
very odd and topsy-turvy about our moral values when we
rightly deplore the one and wrongly ignore the other.

When sex exploits, abuses, frightens or depersonalises, or
when it is bought or sold – especially, but not only, when
children are involved, it is surely evil. But when sexual intimacy
expresses love and deepens affection, and when it strengthens
the bonds between people who have committed themselves to
each other, whatever the legal relationship, and when it satisfies
and fulfils them at the deepest level, is it possible for the Christian to say: 'This is good'?

The source of moral behaviour

It is, of course, true that some of the best behaved, bravest,
kindest and most upright people believe firmly that there is no
God, and construct a consistent morality based on that belief.
Does it matter then, if people turn away from God and Christian moral principles? In answering that, we have to recognise
that it is only in this generation, for the first time, that religious
ideas are ceasing to underpin general morality. Because these
ideas have prevailed for so long, people tend to assume that
the morality which goes with them is somehow obvious and
commonsensical and will continue. Love thy neighbour as thy-
self is widely believed to be a moral imperative which everyone
can accept and try to follow without religious faith, as if it
were a belief which came naturally to man. But, as *The Sunday
Telegraph* warned, this is a terrible error.

No moral doctrine ever comes naturally. It has to be taught,
and it can only be taught if enough people understand the theories on which it rests. *The Sunday Telegraph* pointed out that
what we are seeing now is a diminished respect for the uniqueness of humanity – and the social consequences of that are more

greed, more crime, more family breakdown and more violence – and an extreme restlessness. Although many non-believers dislike these trends just as much as Christians do, they are almost powerless to do anything about them. So what is the answer?

Religion has an extraordinary and unique capacity to keep supplying concepts of beauty and truth. Without religion, few people know what to think, and into the vacuum created pours superstition and fanaticism and pure brutishness. To that the atheist may well answer that the social and criminal consequences about the loss of faith are simply the pain and results from people discovering that they have been living a lie. On that argument, we have to develop a new way of living based on the truth. But, says *The Sunday Telegraph* another possibility presents itself:

> ... our moral beliefs will decay if they are cut off from their source, just as the stream will become a stagnant pool if it is no longer fed by its spring. And that is what is happening in the West today. The injunction to love thy neighbour is not a statement of the obvious. It is a commandment, and one which only makes sense because it flows from the first commandment to love God.

FOR REFLECTION

1 Can we trust God when there is so much evil around?
2 Is it true that moral behaviour has become a matter for private opinion? Are there examples of things that are, in fact, absolutely right and absolutely wrong?
3 In what ways can family life be strengthened? Is it important to do so?
4 What should the Christian attitude be to sexual behaviour?
5 To what extent should morality be underpinned by religious belief?

8

Science, Creation and the Bible

Science and religion

It is commonly claimed that there is a conflict between science and religion. Children are educated in a system which leads them to expect that everything must be tested and proved before it can be believed. Religion does not seem to fit into that category. The Bible and the Church's creeds are perceived to belong to a pre-scientific age, and the more science reveals, the more God is thought to be pushed out of the picture. In a world of science people wonder, is there any room for religious faith? Stephen Hawking, for example, concludes that he can see no place for a creator.

I have to confess at this point that, like Archbishop William Temple, 'My ignorance of science is so profound as to be distinguished!' But I do recognise that the enormous advances that have been made in science have important theological implications – which must be faced up to. At the same time, it is important to realise that science often reinforces traditional views; as knowledge increases, so God reveals more of himself and continues to guide us into all truth.

Dr Richard Dawkins, Reader in Zoology at New College, Oxford, has been described as Britain's most prominent spokesman for atheism. Theology, he explained in *The Times* has simply no basis in scientific fact and thus has no place in the canon of our learning. He has compared religion to a virus – a disease that only survives because it is transmitted from parent to child early in life.

But religion has survived in societies where the most strenuous efforts have been made to wipe it out. For forty years, religion was strictly forbidden in Albania and all evidence of religious faith destroyed; but it survived. Whether the people are taught it or not, faith reappears in men and women, just as music or poetry or the desire to paint pictures is never quenched.

Dr Dawkins argues that we know approximately when the universe began and why it is largely composed of hydrogen. We know why stars form, and what happens to their interiors to convert hydrogen to the other elements, and hence give birth to chemistry in a world of physics. We know the fundamental principles of how a world of chemistry can become biology through the arising of self-replicating molecules. We know how the principle of self-replication gives rise, through Darwinian selection, to all life including humans. And he concludes: 'It is science, and science alone, that has given us this knowledge.'

In response to the comment that the spread of religious belief may be a phenomenon comparable to a self-replicating computer virus, the Archbishop of York replied in *The Independent*: 'With that kind of argument it is possible to explain anything!' For Dr Dawkins it appears that the only worthwhile knowledge is scientific. Many people have erroneously come to think that the only standard for all knowledge and truth is that of science. But, scientists are no more qualified to speak on theology than theologians are qualified to speak on science! In any case, science is only one form of knowledge, restricted to answering only a limited number of questions.

The scientific method of observation, experiment and induction does not, and never can, apply to the whole reality of life. That is the business of the poet as well as the physiologist, the artist as well as the astronomer. Every phenomenon may have a scientific explanation, but science does not exhaust the explanation. Professor Mary Midgley wrote in *The Independent*: 'It is ludicrous to think that science has all the answers; and nobody suggested such a thing until a hundred years ago.' At the end of the second millennium, science furnishes metaphors – but not answers. Science has transformed our world. It has not provided meaning.

Albert Einstein, although he did not belong to any orthodox religious community, described himself as profoundly religious and wrote: 'A legitimate conflict between science and religion cannot exist. Science without religion is lame; religion without science is blind.' The bridging between the two disciplines received a further boost recently when Susan Howatch, the novelist, endowed a lectureship in theology and natural science at Cambridge, and was fiercely attacked for doing so. Replying to one of her critics she said: 'I can only conclude he is utterly ignorant of the revolution this century in both science and theology, utterly ignorant of the new epistemological thinking that has produced the drive towards inter-disciplinary studies.'

In fact, the study of science and theology is one of the faster growing academic areas in the world. Over one thousand scholars in forty-two countries are officially listed as being engaged in this drawing together of disciplines, and there are seventy-two institutions and organisations – among them the Society of Ordained Scientists and the Science and Religion Forum. But the public perception is quite the opposite.

Commenting in *The Daily Telegraph* on the way in which religion and science can learn from one another, the Revd Dr John Polkinghorne FRS, a former professor of mathematical physics, noted that religion can learn from science what the physical world is really like in its structure and long evolving history. This constrains what religion can say where it speaks of that world as God's creation. He is clearly a patient God who works through a process and not by magic. On the other hand, men of science can receive from religion a deeper understanding than could be obtained from science alone. The physical world's deep mathematical intelligibility (signs of the Mind behind it) and finely tuned fruitfulness (expressive of divine purpose) are reflections of the fact that it is a creation. Indeed, it has been said that the most significant difference between science and religion is that science thinks that, on the quest for truth, we are on our own, while religion tells us that truth also seeks us.

It is a widely held and mistaken view that science is responsible for the decline in religious belief. There is very little evidence to support such a view. In the United States, where science is much more part of the culture than in this country, over 90% of the population is religious. Science has not impoverished spiritual values, yet many Christians are frightened by science and fail to see the inherent vision within it. Christianity has never encountered anything comparable to the impact of modern science. If the Church fails here, by not challenging wrong perceptions, not listening to what science has to say, and not seeing science itself as a revelation of God, then it will become as irrelevant as some of its critics would have it be. After all, the creation myths of the Old Testament actually describe a God who operates through observable laws and through the unfolding of human events.

The spiritual guru Bede Griffiths noted that quantum physics suggests that matter is not as predictable as has been generally assumed in our scientific civilisation. Uncertainty has been built into science, a development which to Griffiths seems to open the way once more to the spiritual. He said the whole material universe was a vast field of energies in a continuous process of transformation with matter passing into life and life into consciousness. 'We are waiting for the time when our present mode of consciousness will be transformed and shall transcend the limits of space and time and enter the new creation.'

Science is not a barrier to belief. If scientific education must inevitably lead to agnosticism or atheism, why are all great scientists not unbelievers? Many of the most distinguished evolutionary biologists in this country and the United States believe in God. Many would echo the words of Sir James Young Simpson, the discoverer of chloroform, who was once asked to name his greatest discovery and said: 'The greatest discovery I ever made was that I was a great sinner and Jesus Christ a wonderful Saviour.'

Creation and Genesis

When Einstein's Theory of Relativity was confirmed in 1919, *The Times* headed its report 'Theory of Universe Proven' but tucked it away on page 20! In April 1992, *The Independent* devoted its whole front page to the discovery of 'ripples' in the radiation from the Big Bang. Reacting to that front page news Bishop Bill Westwood of Peterborough said: 'This doesn't make a great deal of difference to me. It certainly doesn't make any difference to God. If anything it makes him even more amazing.'

The evidence for the Big Bang starting the universe with a great explosion fifteen thousand million years ago is overwhelming. The Professor of Physics at the Open University, Russell Stannard, who is an Anglican Reader, has pointed out that the galaxies of stars are still receding from each other in the aftermath of that explosion. We have detected the remnants of the fireball that accompanied the event, and the observed mixture of chemical elements in the universe agrees well with the composition one calculates ought to have been emitted by the Big Bang. There is thus little doubt that there was a Big Bang. So, he asks, does that mean the Bible has been caught out with its six days creation story in Genesis?

The answer is no – because Genesis was never intended to be interpreted in a literal scientific way. Genesis is an example of myth – the art of encapsulating in story form the timeless truths and their relevance for us today. It does not offer a rival scientific theory to the Big Bang – or, for that matter, to the Theory of Evolution by Natural Selection.

In Professor Stephen Hawking's view, one day we shall have a Theory of Everything and we can look forward 'to knowing the mind of God'. But he claims that we cannot think of God suddenly deciding in isolation to start creating a universe. There was no time when this could have happened. Hence Hawking wonders what is left for a creator to do. I find Professor Stannard helpful here. The ideal answer theologically speaking is to point out that the idea of God the Creator has always been linked to that of God the Sustainer. God's creativity is not especially invested in that first instant: it is needed at all times. The idea of God the Creator is not especially concerned with how God got things going in the first place, so much as why there is something rather than nothing. Indeed, as Hawking himself has written from the scientist's viewpoint: 'I think I may find out *how*, but I'm not so optimistic about finding out *why*'.

Jeremy Craddock, a retired forensic biologist, and another Anglican Reader has suggested that the picture of the universe as conceived in God's womb, free to become what it would, and loved for its own sake, is not inferior to one in which the universe is designed by God and loved for his sake. He reflected that when he fell in love with his wife, he had not designed her. 'If I love her for my sake, not hers, then my love is a poor thing. The picture of God allowing the universe to happen, and then loving it for its own sake is one of real authentic love.'

Craddock then goes on to deal with the way in which Darwinism is often seen as a threat to religious belief. He emphasises that there can be no doubt whatever that evolution has occurred and is occurring; and that Darwin's Theory of Natural Selection is supported by mathematics and by molecular biology in ways that Darwin himself could never have foreseen.

Indeed, if we were asked to devise a system to design and build all the millions of species that have ever existed, we should be hard pressed. The information technology used in nature is elegant and simple. The biological world is put together by protein molecules called enzymes. Enzyme surfaces are chemically active and organise biochemical reactions that depend wholly on their structure. The problem thus reduces to that of building enzymes, and therefore, since they are made up of various combinations from a menu of twenty amino acids, to that of stringing amino acids together in the right sequence. 'That is done by the beautiful, powerful molecule DNA, which puts together amino acids in a way which again depends only on its structure.'

Many biologists seek to explain the origin of life and of species by chemical processes only. That 'reductionist' argument is that human beings, and other animals, are biological accidents, cobbled together from bits of their ancestors. The evolutionary process is not moving towards any pre-determined end. But as Craddock notes, 'At the very least, that discovery frees us to love God for what he is, not for the status we had supposed he had given us.'

In 1630, Copernicus' idea that the earth was not the centre of the universe was seen as a threat to religion. Since then it has enlarged our view of God. Darwinism can do the same: enlarge our view of God, and give us a greater respect for the rest of creation – not because God designed it for our selfish use, but because it arose in the same kind of way as we did. All other creatures, animate and inanimate are our brothers and sisters. 'If we really believed that, think what the future of the world could be, not the end of religion, but the reign of God.'

The Bible

A century ago a huge controversy threatened the Church of England. A letter to *The Times* said that things would never be the same again! The problem? A book called *Essays and Reviews* which questioned some widely held beliefs. Its authors argued that it might not be true that all non-Christians would be everlastingly damned; that Moses was not personally responsible for the first five books of the Old Testament (including the account of his own death!); and that the creation story should be understood as myth not history. In other words, *Essays and Reviews* was telling its readers that they were not obliged to think of Adam and Eve as a particular man and a particular woman who were the first human beings to live on earth. When one of the authors, Frederick Temple, was consecrated Bishop five years later, only three bishops were willing to take part in the consecration.

Today most of us accept that the Bible is not infallible. Its authorship is so complex that it is best to think of it not as one book but as a library. It is a collection of sixty-six books containing many different types of literature: stories, poems, sermons, biographies, histories and letters written over a period of a thousand years by people who never dreamt that their writings would be collected into a single book.

It is full of mistakes, inconsistencies, statements that contradict each other, diverging accounts of the same event and conflicting interpretations of the same truth! Long gone are the days when Bishop Usher proved conclusively, by taking every date in the Bible literally, that the creation occurred in 4004 BC! The Bible was written in a pre-scientific age. It is neither a text book in geology nor is it an accurate historical record. Dr Max Gammon put the point effectively in *The Independent*:

> The Bible gives no material proofs of what it tells us: it is not a scientific text book. Thank God for that; text books are soon outdated. Equally important, the Bible gives us no material explanations; it is not a work of philosophy. Thank God for that; philosophers go in and out of fashion. It is difficult to accept, but nonetheless true, that not every question man can frame is capable of a rational answer.

This does not mean that the Bible is not authoritative. There are plenty of accurate details in it. The oldest complete manuscript of the Bible, the Codex Sinaiticus, was written in Greek in the fourth century and can be seen in the British Museum. In that ancient manuscript one can read, in the Book of Jeremiah, about the seige of Jerusalem by Sennacherib in 700 BC. Not far away in the same Museum is a baked clay cylinder, inscribed by Sennacherib's own historians, which confirms the biblical record exactly and describes how the King of Assyria shut up Hezekiah in Jerusalem 'like a bird in a cage'.

In reading the Bible we have to try to distinguish between what is history and what is myth or legend – and to recognise that each can be vehicles of truth about God. The Bible seeks to convey that truth about God, and in that sense it is properly called the word of God – because on that subject it has authority.

In an earlier chapter, we noted the seeming inconsistencies in the gospel stories about, for example, the Resurrection. These arise only because the four Evangelists are themselves approaching the subject from different directions. What each writes is an expression of the Easter faith – and that is how they should be read.

Once the nature of the Bible has been understood, it no longer becomes a barrier to faith. Luther once said that a simple scullery maid reading the Bible in faith comes closer to its message than the greatest scholar reading the Bible without faith. A Christian is asked to do more than simply believe in the authority of the Bible. It is necessary to discover the truth of it in our own experience.

Within the Church of England there is a careful inter-relationship between scripture, reason and tradition. As the House of Bishops' *Nature of Belief* emphasised, there must always be a place in the life of the Church for both tradition and enquiry. The relation between them is not simple and is never settled – it has always meant that there can be a proper diversity in the understanding and expression of the Christian faith.

The Archbishop of Canterbury was reported as saying that if the Bible could be taught and interpreted effectively outside the context of a worshipping community, then it would have been achieved in the fifty years since 1944. That was when religious education became mandatory in all state schools. The syllabus that was drawn up then was largely confined to the Bible.

It was believed – by Church people as well as legislators – that since all Christians have the Bible in common, they must be agreed over its interpretation. Theologians of all denominations were consulted and some very fine syllabuses were drawn up and carefully taught. However, the end result was not a society better versed in the scriptures, but one in which knowledge of the Bible and interest in it as God's living word, decreased as year succeeded year. As Dr Carey put it:

Could it be that because the Bible was taught outside the context of the worshipping life and the membership of the Church, that its message – which comes from the Church and speaks to it – was simply lost? I think so. For Anglicans, the primary location of scripture is inseparable from the *koinonia* (communion) which is at the heart of the Church's life.

For some people, the advent of seemingly endlessly modern translations of the Bible has become off-putting. Certainly there are plenty of people who remember when the Bible meant the Authorised Version – though it never had wide acclaim when it was first published. There were plenty of other translations around. The Wycliffe Bible was published in two version. There were also Tyndale, the Geneva Bible, Coverdale, the Bishops' Bible, Rheims Douai and others. In fact the main reason why the Authorised Version eventually triumphed over other translations had little to do with its scholarly or literary merits. It was simply that the King's Printer and Cambridge University Press had a monopoly on the Authorised Version, and that James I objected to the anti-monarchic notes in its main rival, the Geneva Bible! Only much later was the Authorised Version praised as literature.

But how can we work out what the Bible means for us today? *The Interpretation of the Bible in the Church* is said to be the most important Roman Catholic statement on this topic since Vatican II. It declares that scripture is the soul of theology and that any method of interpreting scripture will do – provided it does throw light on the meaning. No-one ever approaches a text without having some preconceptions.

One of the most off-putting barriers for thinking people who want to explore the steps of faith is the fundamentalist approach to scripture which sees everything in black and white terms. Personally, as a mainstream Anglican, I was glad to see this comment in the Vatican document on the subject of fundamentalism:

Its basic mistake is to forget the historical character of biblical revelation. It treats the Bible text as though it had been dictated word for word by the Spirit. It suppresses the personality of the human authors. Worse, fundamentalism is linked to the 'scripture alone' principle which removed the Bible from the realm of tradition. Superficially attractive, because it offers ready made instant answers, fundamentalism invites people to a kind of intellectual suicide. It injects into life a false certitude.

FOR REFLECTION

1 Do you believe there is a real conflict between science and religion?
2 How do the theories of the Big Bang and Evolution by Natural Selection affect your views of God and your understanding of the Creation stories in Genesis?
3 What kind of authority can the Bible have when it is so full of mistakes and inconsistencies?
4 Is there any point in teaching the Bible outside a worshipping community?
5 Are you worried or helped by fundamentalism?

9

Miracles, Genetics and Euthanasia

Miracles

For many people, the centrality of the miraculous to the New Testament is a considerable barrier to faith. As I have indicated, this is partly because of the current dominance of a particular view of scientific explanation, and as a result, attempts are frequently made to explain away the miracles. But Christianity, in any meaningful sense, depends on the acceptance of at least one miracle – namely the Resurrection.

Both the biblical and medieval ideas of the miraculous were dealt a seemingly devastating blow by Newtonian science – with its view of the universe operating by an inexorable mechanical system. Any miracle would therefore violate the laws of nature. Although, of course, all we can say about the laws of nature is that they are the best description available to us now of how nature behaves. An equally serious blow was given by David Hume and empirical philosophy – with the question as to whether miracles happen at all.

What is not widely realised today is that modern science gives more plausibility to the notion of miracles than would have been likely even fifty years ago. Writing in *The Independent*, Rabbi David Goldberg, pointed out that quantum physics and chaos theory in particular, have revealed chance and indeterminacy to be real aspects of the fundamental nature of things. Such a science is attractive to many theologians because what it does is to remove the requirement for God to have produced a major disruption of the natural order every time a miracle is credited to him.

So, for example, they would argue that it was not God, but a strong east wind just at the right moment over the Sea of Reeds which enabled the Israelites to cross, but submerged the Egyptians. The subjective response of the biblical writer was to praise God for a miracle. That was how he saw it. But the objective response of someone reading the text two thousand years later, and aware of the theories of modern science, should be to seek some connection between the divine will, which is consistent not arbitrary, and the orderly workings of the universe. Nowadays with all the data of quantum physics, psychosomatic medicine and parapsychology, it is certainly possible to give consideration to the notion of 'miracles'.

But perhaps the most astonishing thing is not that there are miracles disturbing the normal order of creation, but that the normal order of creation exists at all! I was attracted by a refreshing article by Margaret Atkins, a theology student, also in *The Independent*. She made the point that the marvel is not that the sun should stop but that it should continue to move, not that a few people are cured spectacularly, but that most of us are healthy for most of the time. The basic miracle is life. If God seems somehow to intervene in the normal flow of events, the proper question is not, 'How can he?', but rather, 'Why does he want to? What is he doing with this?' And when is an 'intervention' really an intervention and not the natural process?

A London doctor, responding to the common objection that miracles contradict the laws of nature, argued that they do not. Miracles go beyond the laws of nature as we at present perceive them, in much the same way as Einstein's laws go beyond Newton's – but do not contradict within their own frame of reference. Thus, the miracles of Jesus reveal to us aspects of reality which are not at present directly accessible to us.

However persuasive such arguments may be, the fact is that many deeply religious people feel excluded from the Church because they cannot believe in the supernatural concepts it emphasises. On the other hand it must be remembered that Don Cupitt and the Sea of Faith, who oppose such concepts, has only a few hundred members after eight years. If talk of miracles keeps people out of churches, then it does not mean that non-realism will bring them in!

The real problem with miracles is not their plausibility but their purpose. If God can do as he wishes with his world why should he want to perform miracles? That is surely a more significant point than all the objections of the scientific material-ists and the philosophical sceptics. In any case, as has been said, we could not have too many people walking on water, or spontaneously recovering from lethal cancers, or stepping out of their coffins. Such a world could not support a species depen-dent on stability.

On what grounds therefore can people claim that the occur-rence of miracles points us to God? Why should one person with cancer be cured when others are not? Why should God perform the miracle of finding a parking place for one person but allow millions to perish in the Holocaust? Surely it is a dubious God who commends himself to us by working miracles?

In the face of such questions, it is important to recognise that there is a difference between the miracle stories of the gospels and the supreme miracle which is the Resurrection of Jesus. The response required by miraculous happenings is one of credulity, whereas the response to the Resurrection has to be one of faith. Faith, with its essential ingredient of doubt, is the only context within which the miraculous can be properly understood as the purposeful act of God. We have to begin with faith. After all, Christianity does not argue from miracle to faith. It moves from faith to miracle.

Genetic engineering

The basic miracle is life. But what about man's intervention, rather than God's, in the process? Huge media coverage was sparked off by the case of a woman aged fifty-nine who had twin babies as a result of the fertilisation by her husband of another woman's egg which was then transplanted. It was the age of the mother that caused the shock, rather than the transplant itself.

Shortly afterwards, there were two instances reported of eggs from a donor being transplanted in order to produce babies 'to order' in the desired colour – one black and one white in mixed marriages. Next came the possibility of taking eggs or ovarian tissue from the bodies of dead foetuses miscarried or aborted, or from adult corpses for transplant into infertile 'mothers to be.'

In a leading article, *The Daily Mirror*, under the headline 'Babies by Design', accused doctors of dabbling in the very stuff of life and prophesied that it will not be long before a 'designer baby' can be created to order. 'It is a chilling prospect that should stir a deep, instinctive unease in us all.' As the *Mirror* said, no-one wants to deny parents the joy children can bring. Indeed, fertility clinics and modern medicine have a major part to play in bringing that joy. But, it asked, is it right to give artificial help to a mother of fifty-nine to enable her to have children? Is it right for the mother? For the father? Is it right for the child?

> Science is in danger of careering out of control, leaving ethics and the law far behind. Responsibility for defining what is and what is not acceptable lies with the Government. It must act with doctors and the Churches to set guidelines. It is a heavy responsibility but one which must be faced and faced now.

Bryan Appleyard, writing in *The Guardian*, warned that for a variety of reasons, primarily economic, human biology is taking over from physics as the dominant science. The real issue, he noted, can most clearly be seen in the words used by the apologists for these innovations. For example, Dr Peter Brinsden, of the Bourn Hall Clinic, Cambridge was asked to comment on the use of eggs from aborted human foetuses for the treatment of infertility. 'If the general public feels ready for it', he said, 'then I believe we should go ahead. If not, then we will have to delay. I believe it will become acceptable, certainly within the next five years.' Tim Radford, *The Guardian*'s science writer commented:

'The problem is that science has once again apparently out-paced society's ability to absorb it.'

Both those statements blandly contain a quite appalling assumption – that we shall all eventually see the wisdom of letting the scientists do what they like. I am in full agreement with Bryan Appleyard in finding that assumption appalling for three reasons. First, the belief that science is, in any worthwhile sense, 'ahead' of the rest of society is nonsensical unless your idea of human history is restricted to the increase of scientific knowledge or you are prepared to believe that scientists are intrinsically superior beings. Secondly, no sane human being can possibly think it a good thing that we should do anything simply because we can. Thirdly, the assumption itself is appalling, because, wrong-headed and despicable though it may be, it is probably right. For the truth is that the general public will, in due course, acquiesce in this horror.

A leader in *The Daily Telegraph* noted that many of the scientists responsible for these new techniques are themselves afraid that science may be moving too fast for morality. Science that is unconstrained by ethics, or which remakes morality to suit its purposes, is a frightful prospect. It noted that the principle of the sacredness of human life is about more than an injunction against murder – it also demands reverence for all the biological processes which renew the race each generation.

The leader argued that mankind should not go tampering with the profound mystery of the origins of human life whether on religious grounds or otherwise. Even in practical terms, the ultimate consequences for the race could be disastrous. 'To put it at its mildest: who can possibly say whether Beethoven's deafness, Van Gogh's madness, Toulouse-Lautrec's crippled legs, even Napoleon's shortness, were not the necessary precon-ditions for their extraordinary achievements?'

In the face of such ethical dilemmas, many look to the Churches for guidance. If the Church has nothing to say in these matters, then has its faith got any relevance at all? Unfortu-nately it appears to be divided. For example Archbishop Habgood was quickly taken to task for writing as if the Christian

Churches were agreed in disapproving of assisted conception
with donor gametes, while approving all forms of assisted conception with the couple's own gametes. (A gamete is a mature
germ cell able to unite with another in sexual reproduction).

In fact, the Roman Catholic position, which goes to the heart
of the matter, is that children should be conceived only as a
direct consequence of marital intercourse. It is the breach of
that norm in the use of the new techniques which leads to a
consumer orientated approach to the conception of children.

But Anglicanism does not take such a rigid line. Bishop
Richard Holloway, who sits on the Human Fertilisation and
Embryology Authority, says: 'We are left with a painstaking task
of examining each new scientific development to see whether it
stands scrutiny. It is a painful process but that is what the human
condition is all about.' There is a huge moral difference between
repairing people by using available tissues and creating them
from discarded germ cells. The root moral issue is the use of
donors in infertility treatment. 'The sad truth is that infertility
treatment by the use of donors does not in fact cure infertility.
It circumvents it by the introduction of a third party. The
key moral and theological objections to it spring from this
third party involvement.' The public debate about infertility
treatment needs to be linked with the debate about genetic
engineering in which issues of human identity are also at stake.

The Independent reported that theologians and philosophers
were deeply divided about two issues raised by the use of foetal
tissue. The first was whether it was right to distinguish between
ordinary tissue and sex cells or gametes which were capable of
themselves transmitting life. This distinction was rejected by
Bishop Hugh Montefiore. The second argument was whether it
was right to distinguish between foetal tissue obtained after
an abortion, and similar tissue obtained from a stillbirth or a
miscarriage. Bishop Montefiore had said that he was opposed to
abortion, except in cases where the mother's life was endangered or the child would be grossly malformed. But he went on
to say that the life of a human being is more important than the
life of a potential human being. Whilst it was abhorrent and

distasteful to use tissue in that way, it was even more distasteful just to sluice such tissue away.

Dr John Polkinghorne, who is a member of the Church of England's General Synod and President of Queens College, Cambridge, who chaired the Committee which produced the Department of Health's guidelines into the use of foetal tissue did not support Bishop Montefiore's enthusiasm for the use of eggs from embryos for infertility treatment. He argued that such use would lead to the creation of a person whose mother had never had a real existence, and that could be very damaging psychologically.

He then raised the important matter of consent. The Current Code of Practice has, as its keystone, a complete separation between abortion and subsequent possible use of tissue. So specific consent to the genetic use of the material could not be given.

The Independent reported that Dr Polkinghorne was supported by the Roman Catholic expert on medical ethics, Professor John Marshall. Although opposed to all abortion, the Professor felt that that should not be allowed to blur the question of how tissue may be used if it has been legitimately obtained, from a miscarriage or a stillbirth.

He instanced a case of someone who gives birth to twins and one of them is stillborn. Would it be right to use the gametes from the stillborn twin? He had no problem with the use of legitimately obtained foetal tissue when it is not a gamete, and agreed with Bishop Montefiore that that tissue will only exist in its own lifetime and, rather than that tissue going to waste, then we should use it. 'But I think family must matter, otherwise there wouldn't be all this hoo-ha about people going back to their roots and adopted children wanting to know who their real parents were.'

The General Director of the Evangelical Alliance, the Revd Clive Calver was, however, opposed to any use of tissue from aborted foetuses. He declared that the use of donor facilities and donor parts in the reproductive process is wrong. Ronald Dworkin, Professor of Jurisprudence at Oxford, stated that moral confusion over the use of foetal eggs, like that over abortion, rests on the erroneous assumption that foetuses have rights and interests. Professor David Papineau of the Philosophy of Science Department at King's College, London, felt that there was a fundamental difference between using foetal tissue and foetal eggs. He said unease over the issue accentuated the general dilemma over egg donation generally, whether from live women or aborted foetuses.

But the strongest words continue to come from the Archbishop of York who has firmly stated his belief that research involving the extraction of eggs from aborted foetuses 'can and should be stopped' because of these unresolved ethical questions. As he pointed out in *The Independent*, there is an irony in the proposal to use ova from aborted foetuses. It is the high rate of abortion for social reasons which has to a large extent reduced the number of babies available for adoption. This has led to the present pressures on the medical profession to find new answers to the problem of infertility. 'What kind of society is it which first kills its unwanted foetuses and then seeks to turn them into parents?'

Analogies from transplant surgery are not relevant. The Archbishop has accepted that sperm and egg donation has already been approved by medical and ethical authorities: 'I'm not saying that we must go back but I am saying that we must stop and stop where we are.' He emphasised that he was not saying that one stopped abortion – because there are cases where he believed abortion to be necessary. He would like to see a gradual phasing out of donation altogether, even though a lot of families have benefited from it. But there are some deep problems that have not been solved about the identity of children conceived by these means.

How important is our genetic identity in forming the basis of our personal identity? From a theological perspective I would want to claim that our identity lies in the mind of God. But the givenness of our genetic inheritance is also basic to what we are, just as our bodies are, and our parents. There are therefore limits to the changes which can properly be made without threatening the very things that make us this person rather than that one.

From a Christian perspective, the procreation of children is literally a participation in the creative activity of God. But, as Dr Habgood has emphasised, '... it is not creation by any means or at any price. Its basis is love. Its means is a sharing by two people of their whole selves. And its result is an intimate relation between parents and their children.' One does not have to be a Christian believer to see that such a concept of the family has a strength and solidity about it which provides a secure basis for personal identity. There is good reason, therefore, to be worried by public policies which might further complicate or erode it.

As William Oddie wrote in *The Sunday Times*, the medical profession cannot be trusted to establish ethical limits to human genetic engineering. He quoted a phrase spoken by one doctor at a conference on medical ethics and human reproduction a few years ago: 'If the technology exists, it will be used.' As Oddie says: 'We need legislation to protect us from such thinking and Dr Habgood appears to have given us a rational line of defence behind which to construct it.'

Euthanasia

In a leading article following the death of Laura Davies, the five-year-old multiple transplant patient, whose experimental treatment in the last months of her life provoked strong criticism, *The Times* pointed out that her upsetting case underscores the increasingly complex question of moral responsibility in medicine. As both the frontiers of technology and the expectations of patients are extended, so the ethical burdens imposed upon doctors grow. Although that particular case gained widespread interest, far more column inches have been taken up by the subject of the legalisation of euthanasia.

Writing in *The Tablet*, Dr Sheila Cassidy firmly contradicted what she perceives to be the common myth that our hospitals are full of men and women dying in terrible agony and begging hard-hearted doctors to put them out of their misery. In fact the medical profession is doing its utmost to control the pain and distress of those who are terminally ill. There is now a hospice in virtually every major city, as well as over one hundred and forty hospital support teams in which specialist doctors and nurses are on call to assist and advise those caring for the terminally ill.

Nevertheless, of course, from time to time patients do ask doctors to end their suffering. Such a request must be listened to very carefully. But it is important to elucidate precisely why someone wishes to die. As I know well from my own pastoral ministry, many terminally ill patients do become depressed but will respond well to anti-depressant therapy. Others feel better when they are reassured that they are still loved and cherished. But there is a small core of people who find their debilitated and dependent state intolerable.

To these patients Sheila Cassidy says she would offer sedation asking, 'Would you like to be more sleepy most of the time?' If that is their wish then she would prescribe regular sedative drugs, achieving a level of sedation that allows the patient to be woken for care and nourishment and then drift off to sleep again. It sometimes happens that such people sleep their lives away over a few weeks or days – but, she affirms, 'I am clear that here the primary intention is the relief of emotional distress, not the ending of the person's life.' Her team has learned that one must be very clear that it is the patient's wish to be sleepy and not the relatives or the carers longing for them to be at peace.

A special and much publicised case was that of Tony Bland, who had been in a 'persistent vegetative state' ever since the Hillsborough disaster in 1989. In their Appeal Court judgement, the Law Lords ruled that all food, water and antibiotics could be withdrawn, and Tony Bland sedated, so that he would die in the following week or two. The Judges based their conclusions on three legal and ethical principals: the sanctity of life; the autonomy of the patient; and the duty of care. A major issue in the case was whether tube feeding is a 'medical treatment'. The courts agreed that it was. The Church authorities repeatedly said 'no'. Feeding Tony Bland was the kind of basic care owed to every human being and was not a form of extraordinary care.

The judgement of the senior Law Lord, Lord Keith, was made on the basis that a medical practitioner is under no duty to continue to treat a patient where a large body of informed and responsible medical opinion says that no benefit at all would be conferred by it. Existence in a vegetative state with no prospect of recovery is by that opinion regarded as not being of benefit. This, if not arguably correct, at least forms a proper basis for the decision to discontinue treatment and care.

According to Fr Anthony Fisher, a bioethicist and lawyer at Oxford, medical ethics – as defined perhaps by a small ethics committee of the British Medical Association – will in future determine law and social policy in this area. 'The search for objective ethical standards, or even some kind of social consensus, has been abandoned. Common professional practice or opinion is enough.'

Like all living beings, he argues, human beings are alive until they die. The push these days to declare people dead earlier, with less of their brains and other organs actually dead, is a powerful one. It is motivated in part by the strain of long-term care on families and carers, in part by the short supply of hospital beds and resources, and in part by the demand for organs for harvesting and transplant.

What the Court allowed in the Bland case was passive euthanasia, or euthanasia by omission. Some would interpret that as medically killing by judicial fiat. As Lord Lowry noted: 'It is not hard to see how the case might appear to a non-lawyer as an example of euthanasia in action.'

The judges did seek to exclude more active forms of euthanasia, confirming the earlier decision in the case of Dr Nigel Cox that a doctor may not take active steps to end a patient's life. In the wake of the Tony Bland and Nigel Cox cases, the all-party House of Lords Select Committee on medical ethics unanimously rejected calls for some forms of regulated euthanasia. Although they acknowledged they had been deeply moved by individual accounts of very ill people who longed for the release of early death, the Lords said: 'Mercy killing would place pressures on elderly and vulnerable people to request it. It also would be next to impossible to ensure that all acts of euthanasia were truly voluntary and that any liberalisation of the law was not abused.'

However, they did endorse patients' rights to refuse any medical treatment, they agreed that doctors should not take extraordinary measures to preserve life whatever the circumstances, and they endorsed doctors' rights to give increasing doses of pain relief to patients, even if such treatment shortened life. They called for improved support for the hospice movement, for more training in palliative care and suggested greater use of 'living wills' – when patients can express, in advance of any illness affecting their mental faculties, their preferences and priorities.

The Independent commended the Select Committee's report, and in particular its prohibition of intentional killing as too fundamental to the law and to society to be negotiable in any terms.

It is rare, these days, to hear such a genuine absolute asserted in public life. And it is very rare indeed to hear one expressed in terms that paraphrased the most decisive of all conservative convictions: that 'No man is an island, entire of itself'.

Among the most significant contributions submitted to the House of Lords Select Committee was the first such joint document of its kind produced by both the Anglican and Roman Catholic bishops. The arguments presented grew out of their belief that God himself has given to humankind the gift of life. As such, it is to be revered and cherished. Those who become vulnerable through illness or disability deserve special care and protection. The care and protection they are given provides a fundamental test as to what constitutes a civilised society.

As bishops, we do not insist that a dying or seriously ill person should be kept alive by all possible means for as long as possible. On the other hand, patients cannot and should not be able to demand that doctors collaborate in bringing about their deaths. That is intrinsically illegal or wrong. Indeed, I am sure it would be difficult to be certain that requests for euthanasia were truly voluntary and settled, even if safeguards were built into the legislation. A doctor managing scarce resources might, perhaps unwittingly, bring undue pressure to bear on a patient to request voluntary euthanasia. Similarly, families anxious to relinquish the burden of caring or even to achieve financial gain might exert influence. Experience suggests that legislative change can lead to significant changes in social attitudes, and that such changes can quickly extend into supporting actions which were not envisaged by the legislature.

In a section on the distinction between killing and letting die, we emphasise that both Churches are resolutely opposed to the legislation of euthanasia. There is a distinction between deliberate killing and the shortening of life through the administration of painkilling drugs.

The Declaration on Euthanasia in 1980 by the Sacred Congregation for the Doctrine of the Faith proposes the notion that treatment for a dying patient should be 'proportionate' to the therapeutic effect to be expected, and should not be disproportionately painful, intrusive, risky or costly, in the circumstances. Treatment may therefore be withheld or withdrawn. But this is an area requiring fine judgement.

Death, if it ensues, will have resulted from the underlying condition which required medical intervention, not as a direct consequence of the decision to withhold or withdraw treatment. It is possible, however, to envisage cases where withholding or withdrawing treatment might be morally equivalent to murder. We are emphatic in saying that the recent judgement in the House of Lords to permit the withdrawal of artificial nutrition and hydration from Tony Bland must not be used as an argument for the existing law to be changed.

Dying is the one thing each one of us can be certain we will face. Those of us who have ministered in hospices know of the welcome pain control, and emotional support they give to the dying. As the bishops have indicated, such support needs to be made available throughout the Health Service. Increasingly that is happening. The last three weeks of my mother's life were spent in an ordinary hospital – but the love, care and patience she was shown was outstanding. Sitting with her, and reassuring her in her final days, when it was clear nothing further could be done, it seemed to me that the bishops' document had got it exactly right:

> We believe that deliberately to kill a dying person would be to reject them. Our duty is to be with them, to offer appropriate physical, emotional and spiritual help in their anxiety and depression, and to communicate through our presence and care that they are supported by their fellow human beings and the divine presence.

FOR REFLECTION

1 Do miracles point us to God?
2 What kind of society is it which first kills its unwanted foetuses and then seeks to turn them into parents?
3 The procreation of children is a participation in the activity of God. What then should Christians be saying about genetic engineering?
4 What is your view about euthanasia?
5 Does the Christian faith have things to say on these and other ethical issues which show that it is relevant to the complexities of modern life?

10

Death, Life and Commitment

Many people, including some Christians, find an afterlife difficult to believe in. For them it is self-evident that when you die, you die. The idea of a life beyond the grave, in their view, rests on a very thin assertion, backed by a few strange experiences which most people do not have.

When someone dies, the body is removed as soon as possible to the sanitised safety of a funeral home. It was not always so. Many was the time when, as a curate, I prayed with the family around the body in its coffin in the house. These were precious moments – not only because they were pastorally comforting to the bereaved but because it helped to make sense of death and its place within life. The veil between life on this earth and the life beyond often seemed very thin.

Today people rarely see a dead body. Death has been marginalised. We live as though we were pretending that death does not happen. It is thought morbid even to talk about death, or, at the very least, it is an embarrassment. If this happened only among people without a Christian faith then perhaps it would be understandable. But Christians themselves often so focus their life on what happens here on earth that they rarely consider the afterlife.

A monk of the Eastern Church, quoted in *The Tablet*, observed that for most Christians heaven is envisaged as a kind of postscript, an appendix to a book about which life on earth constitutes the actual text. But the opposite is true, he argued. Our earthly life is merely the preface to the book. 'Life in heaven will be the text – a text without end.'

Given the way in which our culture tries to ignore death, and the fact that even Christians do not seem to think a great deal about the afterlife, it is perhaps surprising that in 1994 a Gallup Poll showed that more than 50% of the people in this country claim to believe in life beyond death. Interestingly, that is 20% fewer than those who say they believe in God. Nevertheless, with over half the population believing in an afterlife it seems that, however much we may try to put death aside from us, there is an inner yearning about the beyond; and an almost instinctive belief that death cannot really be the end.

Reading through the death notices recently in the *Liverpool Echo*, I was struck by the way in which people were clearly comforted by the thought that a loved one was not far away and had 'gone to be with Jesus'. When comforting the bereaved myself, I have found them greatly helped by that now famous quotation about the afterlife by Henry Scott Holland:

> Death is nothing at all ... I have only slipped away into the next room. I am I and you are you. Whatever we were to each other that we are still ... Life means all that it ever meant. It is the same as it ever was; there is absolutely unbroken continuity. Why should I be out of mind because I am out of sight? I am waiting for you for an interval, somewhere very near, just around the corner. All is well.

But how do we know? Can life after death be proved? Evidence for survival beyond death has been acknowledged even in the *Humanist* magazine, and by the Society of Psychical Research. But, one has to ask, how reliable is such evidence?

There are those who, through attempts at using mediums to contact spirits, engage in practices which are spiritually dubious and often psychologically dangerous. And, in any case, all too often these things are susceptible to hoaxes. But more convincing are the stories from people who have had near-death experiences or death-bed visions.

On one occasion as a parish priest, I ministered to a dying person who did not know that a close relative had just died. Yet she was saying she was being welcomed into the next life by that person. There are also many, apparently well-attested, stories of people who were clinically dead for a short while, brought back to life, and who subsequently recalled accurately what had been happening to them as they watched, as it were, from outside their own bodies. Dr Martin Israel, who has studied these phenomena from both medical and spiritual angles argues strongly against those who see such experiences as hallucinations. All the same, such 'evidence' for the afterlife is, and can only be, anecdotal.

What we can be certain about is that when we do die the process of the disintegration of the body begins. Does anything at all survive? The Christian view, which I find persuasive, is that it is the personality, the thing that is distinctive about each one of us, which survives. But in the life beyond it will be clothed in a totally different kind of body. As we noted earlier, the Resurrection appearances of Jesus indicate that what had survived his earthly death was his personality. That is what his disciples recognised, but it was clothed in a new body. St Paul put it this way to the early Christians who were wondering about the life beyond for themselves:

> Listen, I tell you a mystery. We will not all sleep, but we will all be changed, in a flash, in the twinkling of an eye, at the last trumpet. For the trumpet will sound, the dead will be raised imperishable, and we will be changed . . . then the saying that is written will come true: 'Death has been swallowed up in victory'.

In those verses Paul describes the heart of the Christian doctrine of immortality. It is not, as many artists later showed it to be, a picture of dead bodies rising from their graves or being miraculously put together after they had been cremated. For the Christian, the resurrection body is a new and better one. As someone once put it, the 'message' is the same but the 'transmitter' is improved. Or to use another common illustration, just as the caterpillar has to become a butterfly in order to fly, our body has to be changed in order to take its place in the life beyond.

So, if there really is an afterlife, what is it like? Nobody knows. There is a well-known story about a dying man who asked his doctor if he had any idea about what would await him in the life beyond. The doctor, who was a Christian, fumbled for an answer. But before he could reply there was a scratching at the door. It was his dog. He had left it downstairs, but the dog had grown impatient. The doctor used that as an illustration. His dog could hear his master's voice. That was why he was scratching at the door. But the dog had no idea what was beyond the door, except that his master was there. So, said the doctor, 'Isn't that the same with you? You do not know what lies beyond the door. But you do know that your master is there.'

Such stories can be helpful in underlining our lack of knowledge of details of the life beyond. But there can also be a great danger of being too sentimental. Many of the death notices which I described from the *Liverpool Echo* seemed to speak with certainty that all would be well for the person who had died. That may be so. But the Bible, in several places, gives an uncomfortable warning. For example, Hebrews 9:27 says: 'It is appointed for men to die once, and after that comes judgement.'

There can be no doubt that the theme of judgement runs strongly through the teaching of Jesus and the apostles. He described it in terms of the shepherd separating the sheep from the goats. The clear message in the New Testament is that those who go to heaven, into the presence of God, are those who have repented and have been forgiven their sins through the sacrifice of Jesus Christ.

The timing of all this is uncertain. In God's sight a thousand years is but as yesterday. And modern physics indicates clearly to us that our human concept of time really does not apply on a cosmological scale. What the Bible teaches is that Jesus Christ will return to earth. At the Second Coming he will bring about the final judgement of mankind, of those who are alive at the time and those who have 'fallen asleep'. There will not be an awareness of an elapse of time between the individual moments of our death and that moment.

Inevitably, the Christian view of judgement has allowed the

imagination of artists and poets to run riot! In St Thomas's, Salisbury, where I was incumbent, there is a huge medieval wall painting depicting the good rising out of their graves and going into the heaven, and the damned going down into the flames and monsters and tortures of hell. Among the damned are a king and a bishop – and a barmaid going to hell for serving short measures! Isaac Watts put such pictures into the words of a hymn: 'There is a dreadful Hell, and everlasting pain; there sinners must with devils dwell, in darkness, fire and chains.'

Such ideas, and one must say misrepresentations, put people off the Christian faith. They are revolted by a God who seems willing to inflict unspeakable suffering. Others, of course, insist that the justice of God demands eternal punishment and that this theology is the clear teaching of the Bible.

St Paul, however, gives no clear picture of hell. His only reference to it celebrates its impotence and defeat. In the same spirit, St John's Gospel hopes for a final unity, in which all can be saved and are therefore rescued from such a hell. Matthew, Mark and Luke do refer to the eternal flames of Gehenna, the constantly burning rubbish-dump which was outside Jerusalem. But there the emphasis is still on reconciliation.

It was when the Church began to be persecuted by Rome that attitudes seemed to harden. The Book of Revelation, written against the background of persecution, is an example of that. In fact, the New Testament represents the two sides of an argument which continued into the early Church and beyond, and still continues now. In the third century, Origen emphasised St John's vision of final reconciliation. In the fifth century, this was firmly opposed by St Augustine, who came out strongly in favour of everlasting damnation.

It was this age-old controversy that Bishop David Jenkins took up in his denial, given huge publicity, that sinners are tortured for ever in hell. He also believed that the lurid pictures and descriptions of the Second Coming should not be taken literally. He referred to the imagery of the Book of Revelation, with its promises of eternal torment as 'psychopathic'.

The bishop was merely echoing the views of a wide cross-section of Christians of all persuasions. Not even the most scripturally-based evangelicals can count many among their number who seriously believe that the wicked do burn in hell through all eternity. And a Dominican was quoted in the newspapers as saying that all Roman Catholic theologians realise, 'This stuff about flames is metaphorical'.

Christianity is not the only religion that speaks of the existence of hell. Indeed, some others are even more lurid in their descriptions. The Talmud refers to the fire being 'sixty times as hot as the fire of this earth'. The Koran warns that 'They who believe not shall have garments of fire fitted unto them; boiling water shall be poured on their heads, their bowels shall be dissolved therefore, and also their skins; and they shall be beaten with maces of iron.' Muslims reserve hell for unbelievers. Hindus and Buddhists see it as only a transitory stage in the progress of the soul. It is Judaeo-Christians who are unique in postulating hell as eternal damnation for their own kind.

Bishop Hugh Montefiore, in *The Independent*, at the height of the controversy in the wake of the Bishop of Durham's statement, said that the idea of hell as a place where an angry God exacts eternal retribution from transgressors is very hateful. It should have no place in Christian thinking, despite the traces of it in the New Testament derived from its Jewish origins. 'It is shaming to read in Christian writers about the blessed in heaven feasting their eyes on the torments of the damned.' God wills all to be saved; Christ did not die for the elite, but for all.

Hell is the eternal inability to respond to the love of God. The point about the image of Gehenna, the smouldering Jerusalem rubbish-dump, is that burning is part of the process of annihilation. For the relationship with God to be annihilated is the most terrible thing that can happen to anyone. But that is what comes to those who do not repent of sin. That is what hell is: extinction of the relationship rather than eternal torment in flames.

But will that ever happen? Or will, in the end, even the most evil people, the Hitlers of this world, respond freely to divine love? Many people find it very difficult to see how people who have perpetrated the most terrible tortures and murders can escape their just deserts which, in their view, God should administer. Indeed, some are put off the Christian faith by its failure at this point to preach a fierce message of judgement which leads to the torments of hell.

I find such a message difficult for a Christian to accept, and am helped by Bishop Montefiore's human analogy. He points out that in human relationships we can be aware of human love which it is impossible to resist – even though we know there is no external compulsion on us to respond to it. That is what God's love is like. In the end, perhaps not in this world, God will love us all into responding to him, because it will be impossible to resist him. A favourite hymn of mine puts it like this:

> There's a wideness in God's mercy,
> Like the wideness of the sea;
> There's a kindness in his justice,
> Which is more than liberty.

> There is no place where earth's sorrows
> Are more felt than up in heaven;
> There is no place where earth's failings
> Have such kindly judgements given.

> For the love of God is broader
> Than the measure of man's mind;
> And the heart of the Eternal
> Is most wonderfully kind.

> But we make his love too narrow
> By false limits of our own;
> And we magnify his strictness
> With a zeal he will not own.

The last verse sums up very well what the Church has too often done. It renders its message unpleasantly unpalatable – especially when images such as hell's flames are given a greater importance than they were ever intended to have.

At the height of the controversy over Bishop Jenkins' comments about Hell and the Second Coming, a writer to *The Times* asked:

How many have abandoned the Church and faith, because of the inability of clergy and laity alike to recognise that myth and symbol play as important a role in the expression of belief and doctrine as does the claim of infallibility about scripture?

He was saddened by those who, through their myopic view of God's word, limit not only their own preaching and teaching but also deny to many others the possibility that a different and often deeper and more sensitive understanding could be equally valid and sincere.

The veil between life and death is very thin. Charles Wesley put it poetically when he described this world and the world beyond as 'now divided by the stream, the narrow stream of death'. It is what Christians at the eucharist feel when worshipping 'with angels and archangels and with all the company of heaven'. It is what Terry Anderson described about his feelings when they worshipped in a Beirut cell. It is what pilgrims sense when they visit Iona. Christianity is about seeing beyond the veil, and recognising the truth of St Paul's words, 'If in this life only we have hope we are of all men most miserable.'

But many question such views. Indeed, there are Christians who feel that to pin everything on this life being a preparation for another misses the point. Some prefer to remain agnostic about a life beyond the grave and bring this life into sharp and loving focus – leaving later on to later on. Christianity, they say, is more about life before death than life after death. But isn't Christianity about living with a foot in both camps – in a Church which is alive both in heaven and earth?

Life and commitment

Removing barriers to belief and taking steps of faith is a risky business. Ultimately it is about commitment. We must dare in order to know. The Christian faith is not about a code of commands but a relationship with God: Jesus summoned his disciples to an act of personal commitment not a system of religious faith.

The preacher Leonard Griffith often pointed out that no-one ever learns to swim by reading instruction books, or by clinging to the edge of the pool, or splashing about in two feet of water. The initial plunge into the deep water has to be taken, the launching out – trusting the water to hold you up. Christianity is a faith we could argue about and discuss for ever. But we shall discover its truth only when we live and act as if it was in fact true and risk our lives on its power to support us.

It is not easy to do this in what the Archbishop of York described in *The Times* as our 'culture of contempt'. I am increasingly disturbed by stories I hear from my parishes about both children and adults being derided and even physically attacked for going to church. People are encouraged in our culture to deride or criticise without any attempt to understand what it is they are attacking. 'Contempt entails a refusal to listen and to learn, because the contemptuous assume they know better than those they despise.'

Mahatma Gandhi once advised Christians, 'Put your emphasis on love, for love is the centre and soul of Christianity.' Here again there is a contrast to the culture in which we live. Life today has been marked by a dehumanising process. Writing in *The Guardian*, Kenneth Leech said that closely linked with this collapse of caring is the decline in any real belief in truth. 'As compassion has died, so we have ceased to expect the truth to be told, or to be surprised when it is not.' The problem here is that once compassion and truth have been exiled from a culture, they cannot easily be restored. You cannot rescue spiritual values from limbo as if you were rescuing something from the depths of a computer. 'Once spiritual values have been lost, they cannot be rediscovered without a time of darkness and waiting.'

The culture in which we live is far more complex in relation to belief than most Christians realise. There are many people who really do not believe. Equally important, there are also many who do not really not believe. Robert Browning put the dilemma perfectly in his poem 'Bishop Blougram's Apology':

> All we have gained then by our unbelief
> Is a life of doubt diversified by faith
> For one of faith diversified by doubt
> We call the chess board white – we call it black.

Today that dilemma is even more acute; and simple restatements of Christian belief are no longer sufficient to help people to overcome barriers. Archbishop Michael Ramsey once said that we state and commend the faith only in so far as we go out and 'put ourselves with loving sympathy inside the doubts of the doubting, the questions of the questioners, and the loneliness of those who have lost their way'.

Many people have rejected Christianity because it has seemed to them far too narrow and stifling. In this book I have tried to look at some of the big questions which Christians must face if faith in Jesus is going to be credible and relevant to life today. The facts of faith mean nothing until they have been tested in the experiences of life. The Archbishop of York put it clearly in *The Times* in an article on agnosticism when he said that there are no infallible truths in religion, any more than there are in science, in philosophy, in humanities or in any other human activity. We all have to walk by faith. We all have to use our critical intellects. We all have to pursue the truth as we see it, and be open to truths we do not see. But, as he went on to emphasise, within Christianity this process of seeing, and then not seeing, or rising to great religious heights, and then being humbled and corrected, this hoping and finding hope shattered, this dying and rising to new life, is what the biblical story illustrates again and again.

Growth in the knowledge of God entails 'constant breaking of the mental containers in which we try to imprison him'. Speaking of God is about encountering a mystery – something which we can never fully understand or even discover for ourselves. One of the best sermons that I have heard recently, for those puzzled about the Christian faith, was preached by Cardinal Basil Hume. He reminded us that our culture dislikes the idea of a mystery. We tend to think of mysteries as problems that can be analysed and resolved. But the mystery about God can never be solved. It can only be entered and explored. The deepest reality is unimaginably greater than we can ever comprehend. 'Beyond the limitations of our senses, and even the horizon of death, lies a place of inexpressible joy, the fountain of all life and love.'

Then, in making the point that Christ is the key to making God real for ourselves and for our world, the Cardinal referred to the story of the Good Shepherd 'who left, a bit irresponsibly I think, ninety-nine sheep to seek out the stray'. And he asked: 'Does that not reassure you as to just how precious you are? And does not that word show that it was never a case of our seeking God in the first place? He seeks us first.' God commits himself to searching for us – and somehow we need to make contact.

When we do make contact, we discover for ourselves the truth of Jesus' words: 'I have come that they may have life, and have it to the full!'

No influences have been greater in bringing that new life to enquirers, and indeed Christians themselves who have perhaps lost contact with their spiritual roots, than the charismatic movement. As Cardinal Suenens has said, in the last decade especially, it has affected every strand of Church life – catholic, liberal and evangelical. In a fascinating article, *The Tablet* summed up the life of churches of all persuasions which have been touched by this movement and where people have made a commitment.

- They regard a living experience of Jesus as part of normal

Christian life. They call their congregations not only to
know about Jesus, but to know him personally.
- They are involved in evangelism. Their lives, personally
  and as a church, are coloured by a concern for bringing
  non-Christians to know Jesus. They therefore tend to be
  growing churches.
- They have a love of the Bible and are expected to read
  the Bible daily.
- Lay people are involved in responsible ministries of
  teaching and caring as well as evangelism.
- Many have rediscovered the value of the ancient Christian discipline of prayer with fasting and also the ministry
  of healing.

In other words, this is not about superficial 'happy-clappy-
ness', but a deep movement of the Holy Spirit which is restoring
dynamism, flexibility and credibility in a way which will not only
bring lost sheep home but draw new ones to the fold – and is
clearly doing so already.

If decades of atheistic totalitarianism have not succeeded in
suppressing the human instinct for God, then the more insidious
temptations of Western society will not do so either. In my own
pastoral ministry I have been surprised so often by the way in
which the most unlikely people seem to have had an instinct for
the transcendent.

But for that instinct to become belief requires a personal act
of commitment. At some point our searching leads us to a
point of decision. We may feel there are too many barriers to
belief, too many questions unanswered. So the decision is put
off to allow further searching on the way up the steps of faith.

According to the gospels, the crucial turning point in Jesus'
ministry was when he was walking with his disciples on the road
to Caesarea Philippi. Mark describes how, on the way, Jesus
asked who people said he was. Peter replied: 'You are the
Christ, the Son of the living God.' It was his moment of decision.

If we are not Christians, it is often because we are unable to
make what the Danish theologian Kierkegaard, described as the

leap of faith. Christianity is a way of life. It has to be lived in
order to be understood. It cannot be borrowed by searching the
pages of a book. It has to be discovered first-hand through
the risk of an act of commitment to Jesus. We have to come to
the point where we recognise that in spite of all the evidence
to the contrary, it makes sense to be a disciple of Jesus.

Each of us has a story to tell about where we have reached in
our search for God – never forgetting his search for us. In my
journey it has been the words of a hymn by Charles Wesley
which so often have strengthened my faith in times of doubt:

> O thou who camest from above,
> The pure celestial fire to impart,
> Kindle a flame of sacred love
> On the mean altar of my heart.
>
> There let it for they glory burn
> With inextinguishable blaze,
> And trembling to its source return
> In humble prayer and fervent praise.
>
> 'Jesus, confirm my heart's desire
> To work, and speak, and think for thee;
> Still let me guard the holy fire,
> And still stir up thy gift in me.
>
> 'Ready for all thy perfect will,
> My acts of faith and love repeat,
> Till death thy endless mercies seal,
> And make my sacrifice complete.'

I thank God that his Holy Spirit has led me to commit my life
to Jesus Christ. But I am deeply aware that it is sometimes we
Christians who are the greatest barriers of all in blocking the
path of faith for others. And yet I rejoice greatly that as an
Anglican I belong to a Church which has a spirit of enquiry and
readiness to face up to the hard questions and challenges of our

time, as well as a tolerance and love which gives the searcher the integrity to search freely. So:

> Up then, noble soul! Put on thy jumping shoes, which are intellect and love, overleap thine understanding and spring into the heart of God.
>
> Meister Eckhart

FOR REFLECTION

1 What do you believe happens after death?
2 Does hell have a place in Christian thinking?
3 The Christian faith is not about a code of commands but a relationship with God. Is that true?
4 How can our culture of contempt be met by the message of love?
5 Many have rejected Christianity because it is too narrow and stifling. Why is that so?
6 Is it possible to be a Christian without being personally committed to Christ?
7 What is the story of your journey?